I0380285

How
I
Discovered
My Purpose

How I Discovered My Purpose

A Practical Guide to Faith and Finding Happiness in Uncertain Times

Christine Titih

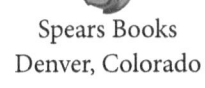

Spears Books
Denver, Colorado

Spears Books
An Imprint of Spears Media Press LLC
7830 W. Alameda Ave, Suite 103-247
Denver, CO 80226
United States of America

First Published in the United States of America in 2020 by Spears Books
www.spearsmedia.com
info@spearsmedia.com
Information on this title: www.spearsmedia.com/how-i-discovered-my-purpose
© 2020 Christine Titih
All rights reserved.

No part of this publication may be reproduced, distributed, or transmitted in any form or by any means, including photocopying, recording, or other electronic or mechanical methods, without the prior written permission of the publisher, except in the case of brief quotations embodied in critical reviews and certain other noncommercial uses permitted by copyright law. For permission requests, write to the publisher, addressed "Attention: Permissions Coordinator," at the address above.

ISBN: 9781942876656 (Paperback)
ISBN: 9781942876663 (Hardback)
Also available in Kindle format

Cover Photo: Karolina Grabowska
Cover designed by Doh Kambem
Designed and typeset by Spears Media Press LLC

To Renee Grace, my daughter, best friend and cheerleader

CONTENTS

PREFACE

If someone had told me five years ago that I would write a book, any book, I would have laughed over the impossibility of it. Just as Sarah laughed when the angels told her she was going to give birth at an old age. But a lot has happened over five years. God stepped in at a moment when I was lost, hopeless and living in mediocrity and turned my whole world around.

He worked in and around me, and brought me into a church family that helped me grow spiritually, which prompted me to start asking questions about my purpose; a home fellowship family that recognized the gift that was being displayed through my write-ups and summaries of our lessons and discussions; close friends with different talents, spiritual maturity, experience and perspectives, who helped shaped who I was to become; destiny helpers that pointed out the way and opened some closed doors; spiritual mentors who helped me and continue to help me in my spiritual development in increasing my knowledge of the word of God; and lastly but not the least, a wonderful daughter whose faith and positive attitude saw me through some of the toughest moments of my life. I am grateful for all that and much more. I consider it a gift to be able to explore all that God has placed within me.

Since 2017, Pennsylvania slogan is: *Welcome to Pennsylvania. Pursue Your Happiness.* Apparently, officials were inspired from a quote in the Declaration of Independence, which gives three examples of inalienable rights given to all humans by the creator: Life, Liberty, and the pursuit of Happiness.

But what really is the pursuit of happiness? I have long pondered on this question.

Entering the US from Germany seemed like an El Dorado. The land of infinite possibilities. The land where all those projects my friends and I had spoken and dreamt about as poor African students in Germany, would soon become reality. A land of open doors, a land of unlimited possibilities. The perspectives were bright. The hope was within arm's reach. The report was promising.

But no one had told us about the challenges. None told us what lay behind the walls - the difficulties to understand and adjust to the system, the roadblocks to gain financial independence, and the challenge to learn and adapt to a new culture. We were totally unaware and unprepared for what the new land would do to us as individuals and as families.

Again, the question comes up: what is the pursuit of happiness? I take a closer look at my life and weigh it against what is considered happiness and I wonder if I found happiness or if I am on the track to finding happiness. I reminisce about the tough moments, the setbacks, the new beginnings, the sorrows, and joys.

My definition of happiness has changed over the years and taken a different dimension. Happiness is no longer defined by owning physical possessions, attaining a certain career level, making a predetermined annual salary, or being in a fleeting state of emotional and psychological gratification. But by something more profound. Something that we cannot acquire by our own means - but which compels us to step out of our comfort zone and to be bold.

In the beginning, I erroneously thought that pursuing a nine-to-five career ambitiously while aiming for promotions was my purpose and I would be happy when I reached the top of the career ladder. While the promotions were coming in, I was happy. So, I thought. Then the dead end. For a couple of years I was at a dead end, performing duties that were unfulfilling. I started to question my own life and what it was I was created for. At this same time, our church started a campaign: *Discovering Your Purpose* by Rick Warren. That is when I started seriously questioning my life. The scales from my eyes fell when I came into the revelation that I was called for much more beyond my current situation.

Then the Lord started speaking to me through His word and revealing to me what he had planned for me. I resigned from my nine-to-five job against all odds and without knowing what was ahead. I started a program to support adults with intellectual disabilities. I found destiny helpers and mentors that encouraged me and led me to believe that I had more in me than was apparent. Mentors, who encouraged and supported me to discover the talents that were placed in me. The start of my business was freedom. Finally, I started to utilize some of the talents that God had placed in me. I started operating by grace to support individuals to integrate in their communities and explore other facts of daily life which was not limited by a diagnosis of a disability. Even as I poured myself out to support them, God was working in me and transforming me to understand what He had planned for me.

I thought for a while that the business was the only vehicle the Lord wanted to use to accomplish the plans He had for my life. Then the Lord spoke again through His word and through his Servants. And I realized that I was called for much more. That the business was just part of the whole puzzle of my life. That I was called to give more of myself than what I thought before. So, I started a non-profit (Oaks of Central PA) to empower, promote and advocate for African immigrants and refugees in Central PA to discover and pursue their purpose.

I finally understood that my purpose was to help others to discover and achieve their purpose through business, the non-profit, and writing. This is my ministry. What is yours?

On the journey towards discovering and living out my purpose, I do not consider myself to be perfect. I am still progressing towards perfection. The discovery of purpose is not an end point but a journey. God does not require us to be perfect. But for us to continue progressing towards the end goal, which is the fulfillment of the assignment God has placed in our lives. Remember, what we do has an eternal value. But we cannot do it on our own - we need God's grace on this journey.

It is my hope that the next pages will encourage you to start the journey of discovering and eventually living out your purpose, which will lead to the pursuit of happiness. It is also my hope that at the end of this book you will get a revelation from God and be able to write down your mission statement and run with it.

ACKNOWLEDGEMENT

Writing a first book is harder than I thought and more rewarding than I could have ever imagined. None of this would have been possible without the grace of God and the priceless encouragement and love of my daughter, Renee Grace. I wish to thank all those who have been part of my support system over the course of the last 5 years and most importantly, encouraged me to write this book; my mother, Veronica Kah Manyi; Dr. and Mrs Koyilla; my sister and friend of 20+ years, Albertine Djeumi; Pastor Frank and Mrs Evelyn Sosu of RCCG Living Spring, Harrisburg; Dr. Sema Fofung aka Ba Shrink; my kid sister, Ella Kehgha; Ni Clarence Ndangam, President of BCA-USA; and lastly but not the least Mr. Ben Clement of RCCG Living Spring, Harrisburg for his consistent support with bible studies. A special thank you goes to the editors at Spears Books and to Dr. Jude Fokwang and his team for their support and willingness to take a chance with me.

CHAPTER 1

THE MILLION-DOLLAR QUESTION: WHAT IS PURPOSE?

I am sitting at a desk and staring at two large computers, processing job applications and entering exam scores. It has been a while since I got promoted into this position and it felt like I was finally on the right track in my career. Then a standstill. My career aspirations hit a dead end. The promotion I had longed for was not providing me with the fulfillment, the calmness, nor the happiness I thought it would. I felt empty and trapped. I felt like there was more in me, more of what I could give to the world. But I just did not know how or where to start.

A coworker once told me that I was a big city girl in a small town. In reality, I was a person with talents buried inside of me, who just didn't know how to get them out. I had endured my own fair share of rough times and sometimes, I had taken a bold step. But after all that, there was still a lingering feeling of emptiness and lack of accomplishment, like there was something I should be doing, somewhere I should be, but everything around me was so blurry. I was unsatisfied and unhappy. And I was not alone.

Each semester, a fresh batch of aspiring college graduates leave college with aspirations of a better life to pursue their dream jobs. How many of them end up stuck in jobs that have nothing to do with their degrees? How many land that golden job only to find out it was not a great fit? How many continue to pursue an advanced degree in the same or a different field with the hope that an advanced degree will open doors to a better and more aspiring career and life? And how many are there with talents and gifts that are simply lost? Talents and gifts that may never be unearthed.

I have always been interested in business. So, I was naturally drawn to pursue undergraduate and graduate studies in Business Administration. Unfortunately, I came to the US just when the world was barely getting over the 2008 financial crisis. Jobs were rare especially for someone with no experience. My MBA degree did not bring the outcomes I had expected. I found myself pursuing a career in Human Resources that had nothing to do with my business degree, and worst, there were coworkers with no college degree that were doing the same job and getting paid more than I was with my degree. For years I felt like I had made a mistake to study business. I felt I should have followed in the footsteps of other African immigrants and gone into nursing or some other healthcare field. It took me many years down the road to finally come to the realization that I was on the road that God had planned for me.

It is January 1st in a church and the word for the year is

announced: Year of Success, Year of Glory, Year of Accomplishment, Year of Harvest etc. etc. The jubilation that follows is deafening and everyone is excited, so it seems. Yet there are some who are lost in this crowd. What would they harvest? What exactly is the success or the glory awaiting them? The year then runs its course just like any other year. By the time the hot sun shines its way through the summer, the word of the year is but a distant memory. Everyone is back to his/her hustling. And the cycle continues. Yet there is someone in that crowd who needs answers; who needs help; who needs to break away from that cycle and discover their purpose. This book is for such a person. Someone at the crossroads tired of the course of their life, someone who wants to be a cycle-breaker; someone who wants to impact lives and leave their mark.

We each have several talents, abilities and skills that have been deposited in us by the Creator. These talents were not meant to be dormant; we have an obligation to invest them, to bring glory to the Creator and Giver of those talents. Only in using our talents in a way that honors and glorifies God and serves a God-given purpose, can we be on the right track in our pursuit of happiness.

In the next pages, I will share mine and others' personal stories of how we discovered our purpose through challenges, difficulties and dead ends. These stories would be backed by biblical passages. It is my hope that someone who is at the crossroads would read these pages and be encouraged to ask the most important question of their lives: what is my purpose? It is my hope that they would be encouraged to search for that purpose and live it out fully. Understanding that the road is not an easy one - it is a marathon and not a sprint.

But God has already given us the grace to run the course.

What is Purpose? Mammy Ly: Spreading Love and Hope to Others

Lydia was her name; but everyone called her Mammy Ly (pronounced Lee). Mammy means Grandma and Ly is a short form for Lydia. She was a heavily built woman with a heart of gold. She was a good friend of my grandmother, and had taken the responsibility after the death of my grandmother to care and support my mom as her own daughter; my sister and I as her grandchildren. We were not Mammy Ly's only "adopted" children and grandchildren.

Mammy Ly lived in an unfinished house in a commercial area in Bamenda, capital of the North West Region of Cameroon. She owned the place and rented the front section of the house to several small businesses. She ran a restaurant in her home and cooked some of the best bush meat soup and fufu in the area. I can still picture her sitting in her wooden kitchen, beside a huge pot, stirring the corn flour. I can still hear her customers calling out her name and asking if so-and-so food was ready. Indeed, Mammy Ly was a hardworking, successful businesswoman, gifted with the skills of fine cooking. She could turn any meal into a gourmet meal.

Besides her cooking talents, Mammy Ly was also a herbalist. She had never been to the four walls of a classroom, but she knew about plants and their healing powers. Runny stomach? Why go to the pharmacy? Grind this or that plant, mix it this or that way and you would be fine. And it worked. She never doubted her herbal concoctions. Neither did her clients. Most often she would rather give away the remedies to those in need than to profit from it.

But there was one area that I felt Mammy Ly had found her purpose; caring for children and youths, especially those that had been abandoned and neglected by their families. Never was the house empty; children would be running all over the place. She was constantly welcoming young mothers and pregnant teenagers, helping them take care of their children, whom she cared for as if they were hers. Mammy Ly never turned away any child. Every summer vacation, there were new faces – some whose families she knew and some whom she did not. When asked how she could take care of all the children, she always replied that if there was food for one, there was food for all. Her arms were as wide as her heart. Always willing to share her love to the abandoned and neglected children.

I still remember one of her favorite songs which she loved singing in Cameroon Pidgin English (Creole):

"If you no know Jesus, you lack something (3x).
You lack, you lack something (3x).
If you no know Jesus, you lack something."

That song shows her driving force. Her knowledge of Jesus made it possible for her to discover her purpose and to live it out fully; touching and transforming lives as she went along. If Mammy Ly could write, she would have written her mission statement as - bringing hope, love, and maternal affection to abandoned children through the provision of shelter, safety, and food.

Mammy Ly's story is just one of many examples of how God has provided us with different talents to fulfil a purpose. Mammy Ly used her various talents (businesswoman, chef, herbalist) to take care of abandoned children. We each have different talents that are buried inside of us. Only in the discovery and pursuit of these talents can we attain happiness. Mammy Ly died in 2003. She had lived a fulfilled life; she had left a legacy in the hearts and lives of all those children she touched over the years.

꙳ ꙳ ꙳

What does the bible say?

The parable of the talents teaches us important lessons about talents - the discovery and pursuit of talents and the recompense that proceeds from using our talents.

The story of the Talent: Matthew 25: 14-30

> "For it will be like the man going on a journey, who called his servants and entrusted to them his property. To the one he gave five talents, to another two, to another one, to each according to his ability. Then he went away. He who had received the five talents went at once and traded with them, and he made five more talents. So also, he who had the two talents made two talents more. But he who had received the one talent went and dug in the ground his master's money. Now after a long time the master of those servants came and settled accounts with them. And he who had received the five talents came forward bringing five more, saying, 'Master, you delivered to me five talents; here, I have made five talents more.' His master said to him, "Well done, good and faithful

servant. You have been faithful over a little; I will set you over much. Enter into the joy of your master" and he also who had the two talents came forward, saying, "Master, you delivered to me two talents; here. I have made two more talents." His master said to him, "Well done, good and faithful servant. You have been faithful over a little, I will set you over much. Enter into the joy of your master.' He also who had received the one talent came forward, saying, 'Master, I knew you to be a hard man, reaping where you did not sow, and gathering where you scattered no seed, so I was afraid, and I went and hid your talent in the ground. Here, you have what is yours.' But his master answered him, 'You wicked and slothful servant! You knew that I reap where I have not sown and gather where I scattered no seed? Then you ought to have invested my money with the bankers, and at my coming I should have received what was my own with interest. So take the talent from him and give it to him who has the ten talents. For to everyone who has will be given more, and he will have an abundance. But from the one who has not, even what he has will be taken away, and cast the worthless servant into the outer darkness. In that place there will be weeping and gnashing of teeth."

All of us were created for a purpose. Just like the master in this parable, God has entrusted each of us with talents to fulfill a particular purpose. His plans are for us to use the talents for His glory. We were created to glorify God with our lives; and we do that by using our talents to accomplish the plans He has for us. Everyone is given talents based on their abilities, the specifics of the purpose or the partnerships we would need to accomplish the purpose.

こ こ こ

The initial step in *discovering your purpose* is asking God to reveal what talents He placed in you.

In the midst of all my confusion and struggles within me, I attempted several options, pursued different paths but the feeling of unfulfillment lingered on. I turned to prayers and sought directions from God. I was tired of doing things my own way, of being unsure about what I was supposed to do, of failing, of disappointments, of helplessness. All this changed when I sought God and heard from Him.

I had always been a believer and a practicing Christian. Faced with the challenges of adult life and single motherhood, my spiritual life had taken the backseat. I was performing the motions of my religion without a real connection or revelation. Then the Lord led me to a church of believers whose mission among others was empowering believers to live out their purpose. It was during one of the sermons by the lead pastor that I began questioning my life. I requested for a counseling session with the pastor and shared my worries and questions about the direction God was leading me to. What was God saying? Why was I so uneasy? Unfulfilled? Was I missing out on something? The pastor advised me to fast and pray and ask God for clarity and direction; and to return to him afterwards so we could see what God was saying. I became too lazy to fully complete the seven days fasting requirement; but I did pray. Over the next weeks, months and years, as I drew closer to God in prayers, He drew closer to me and led me through the process of discovering my purpose. He spoke to me through His word, the Bible, through my pastor and other spiritual mentors, and close friends. This started with me asking the one question; what is my purpose?

James 1:5

> If any of you lacks wisdom, let him ask God, who gives generously to all without reproach, and it will be given to him. But let him ask in faith, with no doubt, for the one who doubts is like a wave of the sea that is driven and tossed by the wind. For that person must not suppose that he will receive anything from the Lord; he is a double-minded man, unstable in all his ways.

When we are at the crossroads of life, looking for directions, confused about our lives, what we should do, where we should go; instead of rushing to the phone to call/text others who may be dealing with their own set of issues and are trying to figure things out for themselves, the Bible encourages us to turn to God first. He is the giver of wisdom. He knows what is best for us and what He has entrusted within us.

Get into the habit of praying first. No matter the situation. No matter what is going on around you. Pray first, with faith. And God will show you the way.

What happens sometimes is that we tend to become lazy. Prayer becomes a burdensome activity. We fail to spend the required time in silent communication with God. Prayer tends to be a one-way monologue where we recite a list of wants to God and expect to have our prayers answered. We do not dwell long enough in His presence to listen with our heart of faith what God has to say.

Because we have turned prayer into an unpopular and time-consuming activity, we tend to rely on others to reveal to us what we should be doing and which purpose we should be following. This gives room for manipulation and frustrations. Manipulations because we end up being fed with lies or sugar-coated truth, but not the truth that can set us free.

After we have received a word from God, then we must obey His instructions. Obedience starts by us succumbing to His will, offering ourselves up as a living sacrifice.

Romans 12:1

> I appeal to you therefore, brothers, by the mercies of God, to present your bodies as a living sacrifice, holy and acceptable to God, which is your spiritual worship. Do not be conformed to this world, but be transformed by the renewal of your mind, that by testing you may discern what is the will of God, what is good and acceptable and perfect.

When we offer ourselves as a living sacrifice, we freely give up following our will, our plans, and our ways. We offer ourselves to be completely and fully used by God, just as Christ did when he came down to earth. Only in the complete sacrifice of self, can God step in and use us mightily for His glory. Remember that we were created to glorify Him with our lives. The only perfect gift is the gift of one's self.

Succumbing to God's will requires a renewal of our mind. We need to empty our minds from all the lies it has been fed. Lies about what we can or cannot do; what we can or cannot become. Sometimes the enemy wants us to believe that we have reached our peak and that there is nothing more we can offer to the world. An acquaintance of mine, a single mother used to say that she lived only to take care of her kids and ensure they succeed. I always reflected on that. Yes, as mothers we have that assignment to lead, support, train and care for our children; but being a mother is just one facet of what we were created for. Before God called you to be a parent/daughter/son/spouse, you are a child of God, with your own unique purpose and the talents to accomplish that purpose.

Also, we need to be free from the need to control the process and the outcome. The world teaches us that we must be in control of our lives. But how can that even be possible? We are imperfect beings living in an imperfect world. What can we control? Can we control what we did not create? Can we control what we have no knowledge of?

The Parable of the Sower: Matthew 13: 3-8

> And he told them many things in parables, saying: "A sower went out to sow. And as he sowed, some seeds fell along the path, and the birds came and devoured them. Other seeds fell on rocky ground, where they did not have much soil, and immediately sprang up, since they had no depth of soil, but when the sun rose, they were scorched. And since they had no root. They withered away. Other seeds fell among thorns, and the thorns grew up and choked them. Other seeds fell on good soil and produced grain, some a hundredfold,

some sixty, some thirty. He who has ears, let him hear."

The enemy of our soul is on alert, watching and waiting to snatch away and attack our purpose. It is said that it is easier to kill something while it is still in seed form. So, the greatest opposition to us discovering our purpose will occur most often at the very beginning. The enemy will use all tactics to keep us grounded and focused on other things rather than discovering and pursuing our purpose. That is why we need to be alert and watchful for the instructions from God.

This parable showcases four ways the enemy uses to distract us from hearing from God and obeying His instructions.

Blurred Instructions/Follow-up Actions

Most people receive instructions from God but then the enemy steps in and blurs the instructions. Consequently, the person tends to execute a plan that was different from what God had originally instructed. Most of the time it has to do with pride. We become proud and run with our limited and sometimes wrong interpretations of the instructions. We are not humble enough to go back to the master to request for clarifications. Which of us on the first day of a new job, has never gone back to our supervisor to seek clarification on a task we did not understand? But why then do we find it hard to do likewise with the instructions that God has given us.

The conversation runs thus:

God: *Relocate to XYZ.*

Me: (speaking to myself. It does not make sense to relocate to XYZ. What will I do there? I do not know anyone there. I will go to the neighboring city. It is still a short distance from XYZ. It would almost be as if I am in XYZ).

I go to the neighboring town and nothing seems to be moving as planned. I am confused. I carried out what I was told to do but what happened?

Me: God, I obeyed you and relocated but things are not moving the way I thought they would. What happened?

God: *Did you really obey me?*

That is what happens most of the time; and so we miss out on the provisions and opportunities that were waiting for us at the location where God wanted us to be.

Lack of Focus

Another tactic the enemy uses is to get us focused on tasks around us rather than on the word of God. We hear of someone succeeding in a field and we rush to get into the field rather than hear from God. Remember that God will judge us on what He has given us rather than what everyone else is doing. Sometimes we get busy with daily tasks when God is calling us to look beyond - to have the big picture.

Lack of focus is the inability to stay committed on one's lane and pursue the course. We get carried away by statistics, forecasts, what the stock markets say, what our neighbors are doing, etc. Lack of focus also comes about when we are expecting to run a sprint and the Lord calls us to run a marathon. Lack of focus has to do with impatience. We are anxious to get to the next thing and to move on, to keep moving, even when God's instructions are for us to be still. We are eager to jump on each new idea and follow it without completing the task we have been entrusted with. Sometimes the instructions for the next stage will not come until we have obeyed and completed the previous instructions God gave us.

Challenges and Difficulties

A friend always reminds me that if it were easy, everyone would have done it. There's truth in these words. None of us really likes being faced with challenges and difficulties especially when we know we are obeying God's instructions. We believe that because we are doing what God told us to do, we should not encounter challenges and difficulties; everything should be easy. But that is not the case. Even Jesus had to carry his cross.

Many shy away from pursuing their purpose because of the difficulties that they perceive they would face. Many are stuck in redundancy and mediocrity because they are unwilling or scared of doing the necessary sacrifice that is required to move to the next level. As my daughter often says: nothing is easier than kindergarten math.

I have come across people who just gave up because of the length of time and the challenges they were going to face. I have also come across those who think because I do what I do, I must have it easy. Though we are not to neglect the difficulties we face pursuing our course, we are not to let room for the enemy to convince us that things would remain the same or to convince us that God's grace isn't sufficient to carry us through the challenges and difficulties.

Deceitfulness of Gain

Many people rush into pursuing a path because of the financial gain they hope to obtain from it. Though we are called to be good stewards of the resources God has given us, we are also called not to be lovers of money or material gain. If we let ourselves be convinced by the tactic of the enemy by focusing on material prosperity as opposed to following God's instructions and running with the word, we will miss out on the opportunity to live life to the fullest. We will open ourselves to depression and other ailments. As it is said in Proverbs 10:22, "The blessing of the Lord makes rich, and He adds no sorrow to it." When God calls us for a particular purpose, his intention is for us to be blessed by it and through it. God does not call us into purpose for our harm but for our good.

ॐ ॐ ॐ

A talent not used can be taken away; and a talent used can be multiplied.

A pastor was illustrating what it means to give oneself to be used by God. He poured water in a glass and then gave the glass to others to drink. Then when the glass was empty, he poured some more water in it.

But what happens when the glass is not emptied? Pride steps in and corrupts the water. The water turns dark reddish (pastor adds something in the water). But then nobody wants to drink the water. Then God steps in and restores the water to its original form. (Pastor adds something in the water, and it regains its original color).

We are each called to serve others; to give as we have received. As we pour ourselves out to others and become empty in the process, God refills us with more blessings and grace. And He gets all the glory while we find fulfillment and peace.

Most often, we are afraid of emptying ourselves, of giving ourselves to others. We want to hold on to the blessings that God has given to us. Forgetting that we are called to be channels of his blessings and not reservoirs. We tend to forget that the glass is *refillable*.

☙ ☙ ☙

Sometimes forces greater than us hold us down and prevent us from discovering our purpose. What happens then? God steps in and frees us.

Examples of these forces and barriers are environmental challenges which we have no control over, poverty, spiritual immaturity, sin, pride, lack of vision, laziness, procrastination etc. The story of Jesus and the donkey is a perfect illustration of how Jesus steps in and unties an impossible situation to fulfill a purpose.

Jesus and the Donkey: Mark 11:1-10

> Now when they drew near to Jerusalem, to Bethpage and Bethany, at the Mount of Olives, Jesus sent two of his disciples and said to them, "Go into the village in front of you, and immediately as you enter it you will find a colt tied, on which no one has ever sat. Untie it and bring it. If anyone says to you, 'Why are you doing this?' say, 'The Lord has need of it and will send it back here immediately.'" And they went away and found a colt tied at a door outside in the street, and they untied it. And some of those standing there said to them, "What are you doing, untying the colt?" And they told them what Jesus had said, and they let them go. And they brought the colt to Jesus and threw their cloaks on it, and he sat on it. And many

spread their cloaks on the road, and others spread leafy branches that they had cut from the fields. And those who went before and those who followed were shouting, "Hosanna! Blessed is he who comes in the name of the Lord! Blessed is the coming kingdom of our father David! Hosanna in the highest!"

And he entered Jerusalem and went into the temple. And when he had looked around at everything, as it was already late, he went out to Bethany with the twelve.

The donkey in this story was tied and for a while it did not look like it was fulfilling its intended purpose, as no one had sat on it before. The owners had apparently no use for it. Day in, day out the donkey was stuck in one place. That is not what a donkey was created for. So, what was happening? At some point in our lives, we have felt like that donkey; tied and stuck, unable to move. Unable to fulfill our purpose. Sometimes the cords that tie us are invisible. They could be words - demeaning and negative words. Sometimes they could be our past, our family ties, toxic relationships, challenging situations, financial lack, lack of education, etc.

I have been that donkey too. I listened to voices telling me what I could not do or become. Voices that sounded like encouragement but really were mockeries. A former classmate once asked me: Christine, what happened to you? I did not have an answer to give. What happened to me, I wondered. What happened to the dreams and aspirations I had growing up? What happened to my ambitions? What happened to my self-confidence? I lost it all. The enemy had me tied up.

What had taken place? How did it get to this point that I was tied up? It is said the enemy takes us piece by piece, slowly and surely. That's what happened to me. I got up one morning and what had become abstract and distant was now my new norm.

Right before my graduation from a boarding high school in a different town in the summer of 1999, my mom informed me of her plans for me to travel to Germany to attend college. That seed of expectation and hope once planted never departed from me. When I returned home after graduating, a harsh reality welcomed me; my mother had lost her high-paying job and had been unemployed for months. I did not want to believe this could mean the end of my dreams. So, I forged ahead, registered at the Goethe Institute to take German language courses, researched various universities, and stayed in touch with our contact in Germany. I never thought my mom's unemployment would last more than a few months but the worst came to pass. After the first year of staying at home and having to stop the German language classes due to the lack of funds, my mother suggested I register at the local university (University of Yaoundé I) to continue my education. But I would not have any of it. I continued to hope against hope that things would eventually turn out for the best. It took four years after graduating from high school, four years of struggle and financial distress, years I saw my mom give up on her hopes of ever having a job again to opening a restaurant in extremely tough conditions before I finally landed in Frankfurt am Main airport in Germany. The psychological and mental toll of those four years had far reaching negative consequences on my self-esteem, my faith, my ambitions, my hopes, and my persona than I would have ever imagined. As such, by the time I landed in Frankfurt am Main airport, I was a whole different person than the 19-year-old who graduated from high school full of expectations and excitement. It took several years for God to untangle the rope that had been tied around me and to set me free to pursue the path He had laid out for me.

Just as the disciples untied the donkey, so you too can be untied and set free from all the forces that are limiting and preventing you from discovering and pursing your purpose. The donkey was set free because he had a critical mission; to carry Jesus into Jerusalem. Oh, what a glorious mission that was! So, we too have a mission just like the donkey but we first need to be set free so we can pursue that mission. Freedom can come from us acknowledging our sins and asking God for forgiveness and restoration; freedom can come from God taking us from the pit to the palace; from a place of lack to a place of abundance; freedom can also come from God blessing us to prosper even in a time of famine; and freedom can come from God speaking the word over our lives and the situation that is holding us captive. Remember that he who the Son sets free is free indeed (John 8:36). Economical disadvantages and environmental limitations cannot stop God's plan for your life.

Conclusion

Each of us is given a measure of talents by our creator. This talent is not meant to be buried but to be traded. How do we bury our talents? Many of us go through life like we are our own masters, living life on our terms, making the rules as we go along. Others condemn themselves to a mediocre life; never having the courage to venture out of it. "This is the only life I know. This is what pays the bills. I have no education. I have no connections. This is what everyone else is doing. I am already working double jobs - I don't have time for something else." These are all the lies the enemy tells us to keep us stuck and prevents us from moving forward.

Some of us are conscious of the talents we have but do not know how to develop them, so instead, we bury them. We bury them by stating all the reasons why it would not work (the master is evil/ the economy is bad/everyone is doing the same thing/ I don't have the financial backing/etc.). We bury them when we listen to the naysayers and others of little faith, who, though might have good intentions, are misleading us.

Purpose is who we are. Our raison d'être. The reason behind why we are on this earth - the lives we are to touch, the contributions we are to make; the service we provide. It is the driving force behind our being. The determining force.

Until we acknowledge and turn to the master who has given us the talents, we will not be living in purpose. We would be living in fear. Fear of punishment. Barely surviving. Never being in peace.

It is said that the grave is the richest place on earth. Why, you may ask? Simply because there are servants who buried their talents and never ventured into discovering themselves and all what the master had entrusted to them.

What does this mean for me?

The good news is that the Master wants us to turn to him and ask him for help and directions so that we can fulfill the purpose for which He created us. So, we can be like that one servant who traded his five talents and got five more.

Matthew 7: 7-12

"Ask, and it will be given to you; seek, and you will find, knock, and it will be opened to you. For everyone who asks receives, and the one who seeks finds, and to the one who knocks it will be opened. Or which one of you if his son asks him for a fish, will give him a serpent? If you then, who are evil, know how to give good gifts to your children, how much more will your father who is in heaven give good things to those who ask him."

What happens when we do not fulfill purpose?

Jesus curses the fig tree; Luke 13: 6-9

And he told this parable: "A man had a fig tree planted in his vineyard, and he came seeking fruit on it and found none. And he said to the vinedresser, "Look, for three years now I have come seeking fruit on this fig tree, and I find none. Cut it down. Why should it use up the ground?' And he answered him, 'Sir, let it alone this year also, until I dig around it and put on manure. Then if it should bear fruit next year, well and good; but if not, you can cut it down."

We have been given the assignment to bear fruits. None of us knows the day nor the time when the master will come seeking for fruits. Today is the day for us to step out and start bearing fruits. Tomorrow is not guaranteed. We have been given another opportunity to bear fruits - let us not waste it.

Ecclesiastes 2: 22-25

> There is nothing better for a person than that he should eat and drink and find enjoyment in his toil. This also, I saw, is from the hand of God, for apart from him who can eat or who can have enjoyment? For to the one who pleases him God has given wisdom and knowledge and joy, but to the sinner he has given the business of gathering and collecting, only to give to one who pleases God. This also is vanity and a striving after wind.

When I stepped away from my comfortable nine-to-five job into the business of providing direct support service to adults with intellectual disabilities, it did not seem to make much sense to anyone, especially not to me. It felt like I was throwing away all that I knew to venture into the unknown. How could this possibly be? But one thing I was sure of, was that I was pursuing my purpose. The minute I understood what God had placed within me and what He had called me to do, my life changed directions. I felt peace. I felt joy. I felt happiness. The road has not always been easy. At times I have wanted to quit. Times I have asked God for a different direction. Times I have wanted to trade my talents for a different set of talents. Times I have cried. Times I have been depressed and anxious and afraid. But in all these, I have never gone back to the past. Never have I once doubted that I was doing what God called me to do. And the joy of obeying God's call is what I think is happiness. So yes, I have found happiness in obedience.

Application

While waiting for God to reveal the exact purpose for your life, you can take the following practical steps:

- *Write down some of the things you like to do and some of the skills you possess. Ask trusted friends and partners to help you list out some of the skills they see in you.*

- *If you are unable to come up with a list because you are unsure; volunteer your time. In so doing, you would be in a position to discover some of your strong points and areas that you excel in.*

- *Give your time to serve others in your local church, in nonprofit organizations or some other community organizations that serve the needs of others.*

CHAPTER 2

THE UNQUALIFIED

How long have you been in this field? How long have you been doing this business/working on this project? These are familiar questions we all too often hear from others when trying to gauge our competence in doing what we are doing. The more years you have been doing a particular task, the more experience you gain to be become an expert; the more people are comfortable to trust you; the more justified you are to have a seat at the table.

John 15:16
"You did not choose me, but I chose you and appointed you that you should go and bear fruit and that your fruit should abide."

Espoir: Answering The Call to Serve When Unqualified
Espoir was originally from Benin, a French-speaking West African country. His father was an Imam (Islamic Religious Leader). For most of his teenage and adult life, Espoir was a Muslim. In 2008, two years before arriving in the US,

he gave his life to Christ. When he landed at John F. Kennedy in New York City in 2010, he had just one phone contact, given to him by a friend in Benin. He called the contact but in vain. The contact kept rejecting his calls. Espoir was confused. He tried asking for help, but with his limited English proficiency, it was a dead end. He could barely speak a full sentence in English. Frustrated, tired, and confused, he started praying. He believed that the same God who brought Him this far, had already made provisions for him. Then out of the crowd, a fellow African approached him; gave him shelter and supported him to settle in his new life. As the years went by, Espoir moved from one low paying job to the next; jobs that required minimum mastery of the English language. He was never able to register at an ESL (English as Second Language) class because he needed to work long hours to support his family back in Benin.

Nevertheless, Espoir continued to have a passion for Christ. He never relented in serving God in his local church in any capacity. Wherever help was needed, Espoir would sign up. Although his English was very limited, he joined the choir. Every Sunday you could see his passion as he worshiped God in a foreign language. One day the Lead Pastor informed Espoir that he was going to teach Adult Sunday school. Imagine the fear that gripped Espoir. Suddenly his limitations sprung forward. Would he be able to express himself accurately? How is it possible that he was the chosen one among so many others that possessed a better mastery of the English language and were advanced in their faith compared to a new convert like him? He felt unqualified for such a calling. What if he was unable to teach? Unable to answer a question? Unable to lead? What if he was mocked at? What if people stopped attending Sunday school because they could not understand him? What if he misinterpreted a passage? What if he misled the people? Espoir was afraid. Espoir felt that he, a new convert, was unqualified to teach people that had more experience on their journey with Christ. How could he teach other Ministers, Leaders and Pastors when he himself needed to be taught?

Nevertheless, Espoir trusted God. After praying and fasting, Espoir accepted the assignment.

I remember the first time I sat in on the Sunday school class. I could detect the strong French accent in his spoken English. I saw him battling with words - doing a mental translation in his head and struggling to pronounce the words. But that was not the only thing I saw - I saw enthusiasm and passion for what he was called to do. He was never ashamed of his visible limitations. Instead he used his limitations as a stepping stone to encourage others. I was the shy type, never wanting to speak up. I would arrive at Sunday school and sit at the last seat at the back row. He would always say, "My sister, everyone has to speak up." And he would literally prompt me to say something. Because he was not ashamed to talk about his limitations, nor ashamed when he made a mistake, this encouraged not only me but others to participate in the class and move beyond our own limitations.

Espoir moved beyond being a Sunday school teacher to being anointed as a Pastor of the French Ministry.

Espoir's story is one of God using someone who was clearly unqualified for a task and transforming him so he could use him for a greater purpose.

～ ～ ～

Have you ever heard the Lord speak clearly to you, asking you to do something that seems impossible, something for which you clearly have no experience? The answer would most likely be yes. God does not look at your resume when he calls you. He does not need to run a reference check. He knows the talent he has entrusted in you and he wants to call it into manifestation. All you need to do is offer yourself to be used by him for his will.

In John 15:16 God tells us clearly that he has chosen us to bear fruits. What does it mean to be chosen by God? It means he has looked past our shortcomings and lack of experience and has seen what he has deposited in us. He has appointed us; we are on a mission. An appointment is a mission to serve and to work for a greater good. What does it mean to be appointed by God? It means we are no longer functioning under our own authority but under the authority of He who sent us. It means He is in control of the process and all we need to do is to trust him. He will fight the giants for us. He will not let us be cast down in front of our enemies and the doubters because he is the one who has appointed us.

An ambassador is appointed by his/her country to represent the country in a foreign land. The success of the ambassador has a reflection on his/her country of origin. When God appoints us, he sets us up for success. He equips us and anoints us with his spirit to do the work. It is no longer us that are operating but his spirit through us. It is grace over grind.

And the fruits we bear are fruits that will endure. Proverbs 10:22 says that the blessings of the Lord enrich, and He adds no sorrow to it. What the Lord started, He will complete it and bring it to perfection. Any business, endeavor or ministry that is established on the principles of the Father, endures forever.

∾ ∾ ∾

Sometimes, when God calls us to a purpose or an assignment, we might tend to look at ourselves and feel inadequate to accept the call. That is what happened to Gideon in the bible.

The Call of Gideon: Judges 6:11-24.

> Now the angel of the Lord came and sat under the terebinth at Ophrah, which belonged to Joash the Abiezrite, while his son Gideon was beating out wheat in the winepress to hide it from the Midianites. And the angel of the Lord appeared to him and said to him, "The Lord is with you, O mighty man of valor." And Gideon said to him, "Please, my lord, if the Lord is with us, why then has all this happened to us? And where are all his wonderful deeds that our fathers recounted to us, saying, 'Did not the Lord bring us up from Egypt?' But now the Lord has forsaken us and given us into the hand of Midian." And the Lord turned to him and said, "Go in this might of yours and save Israel from the hand of Midian; do not I send you?" And he said to him, "Please, Lord, how can I save Israel? Behold, my clan is the weakest in Manasseh, and I am the least in my father's house." And the Lord said to him, "But I will be with you, and you shall strike the Midianites as one man." And he

said to him, "If now I have found favor in your eyes, then show me a sign that it is you who speak with me. Please do not depart from here until I come to you and bring out my present and set it before you." And he said, "I will stay till you return."

So Gideon went into his house and prepared a young goat and unleavened cakes from an ephah of flour. The meat he put in a basket, and the broth he put in a pot, and brought them to him under the terebinth and presented them. And the angel of God said to him, "Take the meat and the unleavened cakes, and put them on this rock, and pour the broth over them." And he did so. Then the angel of the Lord reached out the tip of the staff that was in his hand and touched the meat and the unleavened cakes. And fire sprang up from the rock and consumed the meat and the unleavened cakes. And the angel of the Lord vanished from his sight. Then Gideon perceived that he was the angel of the Lord. And Gideon said, "Alas, O Lord God! For now, I have seen the angel of the Lord face to face." But the Lord said to him, "Peace be to you. Do not fear; you shall not die." Then Gideon built an altar there to the Lord and called it, The Lord Is Peace. To this day it still stands at Ophrah, which belongs to the Abiezrites.

Just like Gideon, there will be a time in your journey towards discovering and living out your purpose, that you will feel unqualified for what God has called you to do. Just like Gideon, you would need reassurances that you heard

Him correctly and that you are on the right track. You would battle fear and doubt and would need to convince others of your assignment.

In Gideon's story, the Lord showed His might in a spectacular way, and as such Gideon was convinced, he had seen the Lord. God might not use such spectacular miracles when calling us for an assignment. He can go through a Pastor (like the case of Espoir), a word from the bible, visions, destiny helpers, and through needs and opportunities around you. At such moments, it is okay to ask God for clarifications. But we must not tarry on the spot. We must step out in faith and do what he requires of us. There are many stories in the bible of God using people that were clearly unqualified per the standards of the world. David was an example; he was just a shepherd boy called to be King over God's people. Moses was a runaway murderer and a stutterer called to deliver God's people from Pharaoh. Noah was 500 years old when he was tasked to build the ark.

What does this mean for me?

It means you don't have to shy away from doing a job, from following a dream that God has placed in your heart because you are unqualified by worldly standards; your creator knows what he deposited in you. He wants to use you. Take that step of faith today.

Application

- *What can you do to build your self-esteem? Get involved in a project that seems impossible, and stick to it to the end. It could be as small as participating in a 3K walk for a good cause, painting that room for a sibling/child, etc. It could also be volunteering to serve in church or a non-profit organization in a capacity that is out of your comfort zone. When you complete such a project, you would feel motivated to tackle bigger projects.*

CHAPTER 3

IF WE GO, WE DIE; IF WE STAY, WE DIE

When the Lord called me to quit a secure job and follow the calling he had for me, I was in a bind. So many questions overcrowded my thoughts. What if it failed? What if I had not heard Him clearly?

People thought it did not make sense to leave a secure job and venture into an unsecured field like business that had no guarantee of success. Did I have to quit? Why couldn't I have the business as a side gig? Why couldn't I be patient/satisfied/content with my current job? Why did I have to be too ambitious?

The story of the lepers illustrates what happened when a group of outcasts were stuck in a difficult position; their options were limited. If they stayed at the gates, they would die; if they went to the camp of the enemies, they could be killed. The four lepers took a bold step of faith and made the decision to move forward. This singular act of trust and obedience led to a great reward. Their decision led to life.

The Four Lepers: 2 Kings 7:3-9

Now there were four men who were lepers at the entrance to the gate. And they said to one another, "Why are we sitting here until we die? If we say, "Let us enter the city, the famine is in the city, and we shall die there. And if we sit here, we die also. So now come, let us go over to the camp of the Syrians. If they spare our lives we shall live, and if they kill us, we shall but die." So, they arose at twilight to go to the camp of the Syrians. But they came to the edge of the camp of the Syrians, behold there was no one there. For the Lord had made the army of the Syrians hear the sound of chariots and horses, the sound of a great army, so they said to one another, "Behold, the king of Israel has hired against us the kings of the Hittites and the kings of Egypt to come against us." So, they fled in the twilight and abandoned their tents, their horses, and their donkeys, leaving the camp as it was, and fled for their lives. And when these lepers came to the edge of the camp, they went into a tent and ate and drank, and they carried off silver and gold and clothing and went and hid them. Then they came back and entered another tent and carried off things from it and went and hid them,

Then they said to one another, "We are not doing right. This day is a day of good news. If we are silent and wait until the morning light, punishment will overtake us. Now therefore come, let us go and tell the king's household."

What lessons can we learn from the story of the four lepers?

God's Word Shall Surely Come to Pass

When God speaks, you can be rest assured that it is going to be accomplished. When God wants to do something, it gets done. When God calls us to a purpose, to invent something, to start a ministry or a business etc., we may delay accepting the call or even refuse to accept it due to our unbelief. The bottom line is that the purpose is still going to be accomplished. God never lacks resources. He is never short of possibilities of how His word is going to be accomplished. He speaks and it is done.

I remember about fifteen years ago when I was being led into fashion, I designed African outfits and started brainstorming how they would be produced. Somewhere along the line, I said to myself, the world is not ready for African ready-made fashion. How would this project come to light? I do not even know how to sew. Who is going to buy the product? I felt discouraged and negative thoughts flooded my mind. I piled up all the designs and dumped them in a box and forgot about them for years.

Then the shift happened. African fashion is conquering the world. Some high school classmates are running successful fashion power houses. I drive down to Maryland and I see a thriving African-owned fashion store selling ready-made, en vogue African outfits. And I am amazed. I had the vision. I had the skills. I was being called. But I backed down. And at the end, what I thought was an impossibility, became a reality. Indeed, with God all things are possible. Now instead of being the producer of fashionable African outfits, I am a consumer.

Many times, that is our story. God calls us into something and we back down. We talk ourselves out of it. And just to turn around tomorrow and see others thriving in what we were called to do. Can we then say our ideas were "stolen"? No, because God is a cheerful giver. He gives to those who listen and obey His call. He is never short of resources. When the word has been spoken, it is up to the individual to hang on to that word and run with it.

The African designs are a reminder to myself that when next I hear God's call, I need to answer and run with it, leaving it to God to sort out the rest.

If the lepers had refused to go, God might have gotten others to do the work, and the lepers would not have gotten their reward.

Your Association Matters

A student graduates from high school and is indecisive about what course in college they should pursue or what college they should attend. During such decisive moments, peer pressure is at the highest. He/she is being tempted to go along with the rest of the friends. At that time, the opinion of the group is more valuable than any advice parents or siblings who have been through the same road can possibly give.

The wrong association can lead to years of frustration down the road. When in college one suddenly realizes that the friendship that seemed at some point to be important and strong, no longer is, and friends have grown apart. At that time there is still the possibility to change course and make new friends. But what happens when the association leads one to study a course in college that has no job openings or opportunities after graduation? What happens when the association leads one to explore dangerous terrains, which once entered can lead to a downward spiral and years upon years of recovery?

It is said, show me your friends and I will tell you where you will be in ten years' time.

The four lepers were friends and agreed to go down to the camp of the Syrians. The bible does not tell us if any one of them was initially in disagreement with the decision to go down to the Syrian camp, but all it tells us is that it was a joint venture. Had any one of the lepers objected to go down to the camp, we probably would not have been learning from them centuries later. But the lepers were in a good company - they were all brave and courageous. Their association, which though was created out of the misery due to their physical state, did not act as a barrier to them stepping out in faith. Their physical limitations did not overshadow their courageous spirit. Together as a group, they went down into the Syrian camp. Something which the whole army of Israel was unable to do, these four lepers did. And by virtue of that, found their salvation.

Sometimes we need to examine our associations and ask questions. Is this group contributing to my progress? Is this group helping me discover my purpose? Is this group bringing me a step closer to God? Any association that cannot answer affirmatively to the above questions is not worth pursuing. Never be afraid to step out of the wrong crowds to discover and pursue your purpose.

Being Courageous Pays

The four lepers were extremely courageous. While the Israelites were afraid to step out of their city; the four lepers had the courage to go to the camp of the enemy. And it paid. When God calls us for a purpose, He never leaves us wanting. The Bible says *the blessings of the Lord make rich and add no sorrow.*

When God calls you for a purpose, He rewards you. Sometimes the reward can be physical, other times it can be spiritual and mental.

Physical rewards are mostly financial gain as was the case with the four lepers. They were able to gather for themselves far more than the food they were after; they gathered and hid clothing, silver, and gold. If God has called you into business, He desires for that business to be successful and for it to feed you and your family and help others.

Spiritual rewards are in the form of the fruits of the spirit. Galatians 5:22 states, *But the fruit of the Spirit is love, joy, peace, patience, kindness, goodness, faithfulness, gentleness, and self-control. Against such things there is no law.*

Spiritual rewards have the greatest value because they cannot be quantified.

In a world where chaos reigns, peace is hard to find. We tend to be emotional rollercoasters drifted by each passing wave. We invest emotional capital on trivial matters and by so doing lose our peace. We base our happiness on external factors. When one of those factors changes, our happiness turns around into sadness. Instead, we should strive to obtain peace and joy that only comes from God, based on our trust and faith in Him.

Proverbs 28:1:1 says, *"But the righteous are as bold as a*

lion."

We are called to be bold and courageous. When we accept Christ as our Lord and personal Savior, the Holy Spirit grants us the grace to be bold. Boldness is required to be able to step out and do what the Lord assigned for us. When we are righteous, we are as bold as a lion through Jesus Christ and by the Holy Spirit manifesting in our lives.

The importance of being bold, courageous or strong as we pursue our God-given purpose cannot be over-overemphasized.

After Moses died and God called Joshua to lead the Israelites (Joshua 1); it was a tough call for Joshua. He had seen firsthand the stubbornness of the Israelites and the challenges that Moses had faced since bringing them out of Egypt. Anyone in his place would be fearful. But when God called him, God told him several times to "be strong and courageous" (verse 6) and "only be strong and very courageous" (verse 7). Why would God repeat to Joshua that he needed to be bold, strong, and courageous? Because fear can hold you tight and prevent you from pursuing your purpose. Being bold requires faith and trust that God is in control. But boldness does not just come naturally. In the book of Acts 4, the believers understood they needed to pray for boldness to survive in an era of confusion and persecution after the death of Jesus.

The Believers Pray for Boldness: Acts 4: 23-31

> When they were released, they went to their friends and reported what the chief priests and the elders had said to them. And when they heard it, they lifted their

voices together to God and said, "Sovereign Lord, who made the heaven and the earth and the sea and everything in them, who through the mouth of our father David, your servant, said by the Holy Spirit, "'Why did the Gentiles rage, and the peoples plot in vain? The kings of the earth set themselves, and the rulers were gathered together against the Lord and against his Anointed' for truly in this city there were gathered together against your holy servant Jesus, whom you anointed, both Herod and Pontius Pilate, along with the Gentiles and the people of Israel, to do whatever your hand and your plan had predestined to take place. And now, Lord, look upon their threats and grant to your servants to continue to speak your word with all boldness, while you stretch out your hand to heal, and signs and wonders are performed through the name of your holy servant Jesus." And when they had prayed, the place in which they were gathered together was shaken, and they were all filled with the Holy Spirit and continued to speak the word of God with boldness.

After the death and resurrection of Jesus, the disciples were being persecuted, jailed, and threatened by the authorities, as they proclaimed the good news. Fear naturally gripped them but instead of succumbing to fear and doing its bidding, they turned their attention to God and prayed for boldness to continue to do His will. Their prayer was answered by God and the Holy Spirit was given to them so they could continue preaching the good news with boldness.

There is a battle taking place when we are on the track to

pursue the purpose God has in our lives. We cannot expect it to be easy. It is a battle that is fought spiritually, mentally, and physically. The mental aspect of it has to do with the state of our minds - how steadfast are we? How do we cope with challenges on the way? How do we react when things do not seem to go the way we expect?

The pursuit of our purpose requires us to be bold.

Joshua 1:9

> Yes, be bold and strong! Banish fear and doubt! For remember, the Lord your God is with you wherever you go.

We sometimes think that because God has given us a word and a promise, we do not have a part to play. We think it would be easy, but it is a battle and this battle requires us to be bold and strong. We need to grow into the role that God has called us to be. We need a complete transformation of our mind. We need to be bold.

God does not leave us alone. He gives us freely the Holy Spirit who, just as he gave boldness to the disciples, will give us boldness to do the works God predestined for us to do. Do not be your own limitation

Sometimes we get stuck in a rut. Going neither forward nor backwards. And we are content to dwell in this state of mediocrity. Sometimes the limitations to the pursuit of our purpose is not from outside, it is from within.

A popular quote from Henry Ford goes thus, "Whether you think you can, or you think you can't, you're right." We can be our strongest supporter or our fiercest opponent. We can convince and push ourselves to perform an impossible and insurmountable task. As well as discourage ourselves from performing the same tasks. When we become at ease in our comfort zones, we can find strong reasons for not pursuing our purpose, especially if there are roadblocks on the way.

෯ ෯ ෯

Be a Destiny Helper

When the four lepers had their fill, they decided to share the good news to the rest of Israel who was languishing in hunger and fear.

A friend once said that the sky is too wide for all the birds to fly in it. We sometimes hold off on assisting others to discover their purpose or to fulfill their purpose because we perceive them as competition. Sometimes, we selfishly hold on to information because we do not see why the other party should get information easily when we had to toil to get the same information. The reality is that the sky is indeed too big for all the birds to fly in it.

If we understand the uniqueness of purpose, then we will have no reason to be envious or jealous of another person pursuing their purpose or withhold information that could be beneficial to them on their journey. Each person has their specific purpose based on the unique set of talents that God has placed in each of them. As distinct as are the lines on our palms, so are our purposes. We are called to help one another, to mentor and lead the way for someone else to achieve their purpose. Because at the end of it all, it is not about us or them but about God and His will.

The will of God will ultimately be accomplished with or without us playing our part. But what a blessing it is to be a part of God's plan. To obey His instructions and show the way to others to follow. The four lepers understood that to obey God and be in His will, they needed to share the good news with others and lead the way. They understood the significance of what just took place, that is was not by their might but by God's.

Holding on to information and refusing to share it with others and to show the way to others, is a sign of pride; this leads us to think that what we accomplished is due to our own power. It is refusing to be humble and acknowledge that we owe all that we have accomplished so far to a power greater than us. It is also believing that we can control and determine what will happen to others. The truth remains that the will of God will be accomplished. Be a part of that will and show someone else the way.

ѣ ѣ ѣ

In the first year of operating my business, things were extremely slow. I had only one client whom I supported in their home. I had marketed the business on several fronts but in vain. For a long while it seemed like I had hit a dead end. I was becoming frustrated. Especially as other businesses in the same field were seemingly getting all the leads. I was not able to penetrate the market.

A friend from my local church, who also happened to be the church's business group leader, informed me of a business opportunity. A giant was closing some segments of its business. This was an opportunity for another business to step in and provide these services as the need was high. At first, I was suspicious and reluctant. If there was a need for the services, why wasn't this friend doing the business himself? Who sees an opportunity and forgoes it? Then this friend suggested we survey the businesses that were providing services in the area. So, we drove around and observed how the services were being provided by other agencies. He went further to introduce me to a contact who had worked with the giant for years. This contact proved to be extremely crucial in the first months as I ventured into this new segment.

This friend became my destiny helper; God used him to point me to the path He wanted me to follow. What would have happened if the friend had disobeyed the instructions and kept the information to himself? Or even pursued the opportunity for himself? There's blessing in helping others to discover and pursue their purpose. The reason why the story of the four lepers is known today is because they went back and informed the whole Israel of what the Lord had done. Had they not done that; their story would probably not have been known.

So too this friend was playing his own role in the will of God. He was sharing information and pointing the way, though he himself could have made a profit from the business opportunity.

We should all be willing to step in and support others, according to God's will and instructions. The sky is indeed too big for all the birds to fly in it.

What does this mean for me?

There comes a point in time when we must make the decision to resist mediocrity and pursue our purpose, a time in our lives, when we make the bold decision to step out in faith, trusting that God has it under control. Until we take that decision and take that bold step of faith, we will be at the gate, living in mediocrity and spinning on the wheels; we would not experience the full extent of the life that God has in store for us.

Many find themselves living paycheck to paycheck and stuck in jobs that lead nowhere. The fear of failure and the uncertainty about the future holds them bound and stuck in a rut.

Make the decision today to not be that person any longer. Jeremiah 6:16a says:

> Thus, says the Lord; "Stand by the roads, and look, and ask for the ancient path, where the good way is; and walk in it, and find rest for your souls."

The good news is that we do not have to work it out on our own. The Lord is willing to direct us and show us the path to follow. He is calling out to us; and all we must do is to ask directions from him, and He guarantees us that we will find rest for our souls when we walk in it.

Application

- *Look at your inner circle? Who are you following? Are they leading you on the right path? Disassociate yourself from toxic friendships. Look around in your church, college, job site; is someone there living out their purpose? Connect with them.*

- *Remember that having bold friends can prompt us to be bold as well.*

CHAPTER 4

PERFECT LOVE CASTS OUT ALL FEAR

Have you ever been so afraid and unable to breathe? You are doing a normal activity, daily chores; nothing much to worry about. Your mind is at peace. Or so you think. Then one phone call, one text message, one idle thought, one email message and you are suddenly having palpitations and fear grips hold of you. The next minutes and hours are a battlefield of the mind.

We all have faced fear in our lives at one point or another. For some of us, fear hinges around us constantly, like an invisible garment. Some of us are aware and self-conscious that we are afraid. But some of us are too proud and scared to admit that fear has held us captive. So, we display a false appearance of having all under control and a false sense of faith; faith without a foundation.

Fear paralyzes and blinds us. Fear does not see beyond today. It magnifies every detail and makes us turn into wrong conclusions. Fear makes us unable to see opportunities and as such are blinded by the obstacles. Fear makes us overreact to everything and anything. Fear is a spirit that follows us like a shadow waiting to creep in and stay, if we open the door for it.

It is okay to feel fear, but we do not need to remain in a state of fear.

Ama: When Fear of Uncertainty Holds You Back From Pursuing Purpose

Ama had always been interested in going into business. For years she would contact me requesting information about different business ventures, and I would support as needed. I encouraged her to venture into business, if that was what God was calling her to do. I shared my challenges and difficulties. Although Ama was persuaded God was leading her to start a business, year in and year out, she never made that initial step to launch out. What Ama never shared was that she was afraid. Afraid of starting and failing. I felt sharing my experiences could serve as an encouragement to her. But what Ama saw were the challenges, not God's grace to overcome the challenges.

Then coronavirus hit the US in March 2020, and many businesses, including mine were led to temporarily shut down. Ama said, "Christine, who would have known? Now see your business is shut down. If I had started mine, it would have been shut down too."

Fear had succeeded in convincing Ama all these years that it was too difficult to launch her own business; and now fear was convincing her that her decision was right. What Ama did not know was that even during this season, new businesses were being launched. Some for the first time; and some as part of a diversification plan. The season also provided an opportunity for some people to learn and acquire new skills; revisit their business operations and develop more effective strategies; and spending more time with God to learn what was their purpose.

Fear is gripping; and it can cloud our vision and amplify what we focus on. What are you focusing on? Shadows can make an object look bigger than what it really is. Fear can make opportunities look like obstacles; an open door look like a closed one; a pathway look like a dead end; and an extended hand of help look like a trap. Make sure you are not looking at the shadows and letting fear prevent you from launching out into what God has called you to do.

Joseph: When Your Past Success Paralyzes You

Joseph was a successful entrepreneur with many business ventures in the real estate and hospitality industries. He was viewed as a leader in his community as he was among the first African immigrants in his community to launch into business. For about 10 years, Joseph had known immense success and recognition in business. His role in the community could not be neglected. Everyone wanted to start a business just seeing how successful Joseph was. Many turned to him for advice and information before starting a business; they would run their ideas to him to get his feedback.

Then the coronavirus shutdown the US and businesses like Joseph's were shut down and took a hit.

During the first early weeks of the shutdown, Joseph became an image of his past self. He had been hit hard-just like the rest of the community. But Joseph was taking it worse than others. He was afraid; and the fear could be seen all over him. He was losing his role as a community leader during the crisis due to fear. He became negative, not seeing a way out. Weeks in and weeks out, it was not looking like he was coming out of the downward spiral; Joseph was afraid. His faith had been based on the success of his business. When that was taken away from him, he was lost. Fear held him captive. Fear deprived him of the opportunity to rise during this crisis and lead and encourage others. Fear deprived him of his testimony and an opportunity to perform good works in the lives of others in the community who were looking unto him, especially during such difficult moments.

ॐ ॐ ॐ

Like Joseph, we too can become afraid when it appears like we are losing control over a situation or over our lives. When we are in such a state, we are unable to look beyond the current issue at hand. Fear prevents us from seeing a solution to our problems. Fear can hold us hostage and prevent us from discovering and pursing our purpose.

How can we prevent fear from taking us hostage?

The Bible says in 1 John:18 that "There is no fear in love. But perfect love drives out fear because fear has to do with punishment. The one who fears is not made perfect in love."

What does this mean? Whose love are we talking about? What is this love that can make me feel whole again? What is this love that can make me live a purpose-filled life and a peaceful life; a life that I am not under the influence of my emotions and the inevitabilities of life?

The answer lies in the perfect love of God through His Son, Jesus Christ, who gave His life for you and me. He says in John 14:27: "Peace I leave with you; my peace I give you. Not as the world gives, do I give you. Let not your hearts be troubled, neither let them be afraid."

His peace comforts us and lifts our broken spirits. When we rest in His peace, fear has no place in us. This peace cannot be found anywhere else but in Him and through Him. It is a gift. Accept it today!

No matter where you have been, no matter what you have done, He is knocking at your door (Revelations 3:20), waiting to envelope you with His love. He is willing to take you just as you are, with your past, with your shortcomings and failures, and with your mistakes, simply because He loves you.

You do not have to dwell in fear. You do not have to feel hopeless and move along life like an emotional rollercoaster. Do not let fear paralyze you and keep you a prisoner. Let the love of God penetrate your being and transform you and set you free. Let His love comfort you and strengthen you. There is no love like His.

Accept His perfect love today and be made whole again!

ॐ ॐ ॐ

When we are called to discover and pursue our purpose, there will always be instances where we experience fear. Fear would try to tame us and prevent us from launching out. We must not give in to it but must fight it with faith; faith not in our possessions and the economy, but faith in God, who loves us and promises never to leave us alone.

Although my business was shut down due to the coronavirus, I never regretted having accepted the call from God to start the business in the first place. Because my faith was not in the business but in God. I decided not to look at the resource (business) but at the source (God). We might have been surprised by the coronavirus, but God was not. Before a disaster strikes, God has already provided provisions and a way out for His children.

Application

What to do when you are afraid to carry out an assignment.

- *First, admit that it is okay to feel fear. Write your fears down. Be as specific as possible. Sometimes when we write things down, we can approach them from a better perspective. For each fear item, write down why you are afraid and how it could be resolved.*

- *Second, do it anyway. Break down the tasks into smaller steps.*

- *As you step out to do it, God's grace is available for you.*

- *Remember it is okay to feel fear.*

CHAPTER 5

WORDS HAVE LIFE

My childhood was marked by the fear of words in the form of curses. One was afraid to offend the parents, uncles, aunts, the old grandmother in the village, the elder in the family etc. for fear of being cursed by their words. We all understood the power of those words. They paralyzed you as soon as they were spoken, and they haunted you for years. I was headstrong when growing up. I was never scared of speaking up, a totally unacceptable character when growing up in an African culture. Several times my elder sister would caution me to be silent: "Titih, do you want to be cursed. Keep quiet. Be careful." She did not want me to fall under the power of those curses by a parent or family member.

Sometimes the words were not intended to be curses; nevertheless, they carried a negative connotation. I remember an argument with my mom - I was about 19 at the time. My mom was complaining about the fact that I was an introvert. She said, "Christine, one day you will sit in your home and talk to the chairs." A simple sentence, yet a powerful one. The words took hold of my life and haunted me for a long time and later, when I was going through a separation, I found myself alone talking to my chairs.

Indeed, words have life when we choose to give it to them.

ॐ ॐ ॐ

In November 2019, one of my Pastors texted me about a revelation - there would be a sudden death in my family and that I should pray and fast. This revelation came just days after the second anniversary of the death of my young cousin who had died giving birth to twins. The death was sudden, painful and a great shock to the entire family. I had shared this sad event with many in my inner and church circles at that time, including this Pastor.

My family history had been marred with sudden deaths, and most often, preventable deaths. The pain of the past was real, and the hurt of lost family members was still raw in my soul. My mom had lost her mother at barely 39 years to unknown circumstances - which was later attributed to heart-related issues. And my mom had grown up with the fear that she might not live past her mother's age. Unbeknownst to us all, that fear had gripped my family and I was not immune to it.

So, when I got the message from this Pastor, my first reaction was pain, fear, and confusion. The words sank in my heart and took life. I could barely breathe. I started having palpitations and imagining the worst. My heart skipped a beat each time the phone rang, for I was scared it was bad news. Fear had taken hold of me and I could do nothing but sit back and watch it do its bidding. Days went by and I was in a constant state of fear. A friend called to inquire what was going on with me. After sharing what the Pastor told me, the friend suggested prayers. We started praying and as we were praying, I felt peace and the chains falling off my heat. At that point, a passage from the bible hit my spirit:

Romans 8: 37-39

> No, in all these things we are more than conquerors through him who loved us. For I am sure that nei-ther death nor life, nor angels nor rulers, nor things present nor things to come nor powers, nor height nor depth, nor anything else in all creation, will be able to separate us from the love of God in Christ Jesus our Lord.

This word from the Lord gave me strength and renewed my hope. I was confident that God was in control and that nothing could ever separate me from His love. I texted the passage to the Pastor and never heard another word again about the so-called revelation. I moved on with my life and no sudden deaths occurred. One thing I learned from this experience was that words have only as much power as we give to them. The more we accept and dwell on those words, the more they keep us captive and become alive. The moment we hear a word that is contrary to what God says about us, we need to pray over it and reject it. Let the only word that shapes our lives be what God says about us in His word.

Apart from fearing curses, we also grew up fearing to

share good news with family members, acquaintances, or friends, for fear that they could prevent the good news from materializing. A cousin got her visa to travel abroad, and her parents cautioned her not to share the news to an aunt or uncle; or run the risk of not travelling. Someone got a job and did not share the news to family and friends for fear of losing the job. So, we grew up suspecting everyone and anybody about their potential to turn our good tidings to something evil or worse.

There is a story in the bible that illustrates the power of spoken words.

Zechariah and John the Baptist: Luke 1: 8-22

Now while he was serving as priest before God when his division was on duty, according to the custom of the priesthood, he was chosen by lot to enter the temple of the Lord and burn incense. And the whole multitude of the people were praying outside at the hour of incense. And there appeared to him an angel of the Lord standing on the right side of the altar of incense. And Zechariah was troubled when he saw him, and fear fell upon him. But the angel said to him, "Do not be afraid, Zechariah, for your prayer has been heard, and your wife Elizabeth will bear a son, and you shall call his name John. And you will have joy and gladness, and many will rejoice at his birth, for he will be great before the Lord. And he must not drink wine or strong drink, and he will be filled with the Holy Spirit, even from his mother's womb. And he will turn many of the children of Israel to the Lord their God, and he will go before him in spirit and power of Elijah, to turn the hearts of the fathers to the children, and the disobedient to the wisdom of the just, to make ready for the Lord a people prepared."

And Zechariah said to the angel, "How shall I know this? For I am an old man, and my wife is advanced in years." And the angel answered him, "I am Gabriel. I stand in the presence of God, and I was sent to speak to you and to bring this good news. And behold, you will be silent and unable to speak until the day that these things take place, because you did not believe my words, which will be fulfilled in their time." And the people were waiting for Zechariah, and they were wondering at his delay in the temple. And when he came out, he was unable to speak to them, and they realized that he had seen a vision in the temple. And he kept making sounds to them and remained mute.

Zechariah and his wife Elizabeth were advanced in age and did not have any children. When the angel came to Zechariah with the Word, he doubted how it would come to pass. He doubted how it would be physically possible for his wife to bear a child. Due to his unbelief, the angel said he was not going to speak until the fulfillment of the word.

Why couldn't Zechariah speak? Because words carry power. Remember that God created the world with the word. He spoke and it took place. Faith-filled and fear-filled words carry power. They bring into existence whatever force behind them. When you speak out of fear and unbelief, you create a situation of fear. When you speak words of faith and power, they create likewise.

When God gives us a word, we have the choice to believe or to doubt. And out of the rivers of our hearts the words flow. If we are filled with doubt, we start saying words just like what Zechariah said. We allow our unbelief to take the form of words and come to life.

Words are powerful tools and should not be taken for granted.

What does this mean for me? How then are we to respond to a word from God?

The story of the angel's visitation to Mary is an example of how to speak words of faith in a difficult situation. In this passage we see how Mary's answer to the message from the angel differs from that of Zechariah.

The Announcement of the Birth of Jesus: Luke 1:26-38

> In the sixth month the angel Gabriel was sent from God to a city of Galilee named Nazareth, to a virgin betrothed to a man whose name was Joseph, of the house of David. And the virgin's name was Mary. And he came to her and said, "Greetings, o favored one, the Lord is with you!" But she was greatly troubled at the saying and tried to discern what sort of greeting this might be. And the angel said to her, "Do not be afraid, Mary, for you have found favor with God. And behold, you will conceive in your womb and bear a son, and you shall call his name Jesus. He will be great and will be called the Son of the Most High. And the Lord God will give him the throne of his father David, and he will reign over the house of Jacob forever, and

his kingdom there will be no end."

And Mary said to the angel, "How will this be, since I am a virgin?"

And the angel answered her, "The Holy Spirit will come upon you, and the power of the Most High will overshadow you, therefore the child to be born will be called holy - the Son of God. and behold, your relative Elizabeth in her old age has also conceived a son, and this is the sixth month with her who was called barren. For nothing will be impossible with God."

And Mary said, "Behold, I am the servant of the Lord, let it be to me according to your word."

And the angel departed from her.

We are all familiar with the story of the virgin birth of Jesus. While most interpretations concentrate on the message of the angel, let us look at the response of Mary.

This story is not just about the birth of Jesus, but it is also a story of Purpose - Mary's Purpose and how she responded to the call from God. Contrary to Zechariah who after expressing the difficulty and the challenges involved, dwelled in his unbelief, and was consequently rendered mute to prevent any further hindrance to the fulfilment of the prophesy.

Mary on the other hand did not dwell on her unbelief; she let go of her unbelief and made the decision to dwell in faith. She spoke words of faith; words that we all need to speak when we hear the call of the Lord.

Send me Lord, here I am. My life does not belong to me anymore. Let your will be done. Let it be done to me as you have said.

These words carry life, they carry grace; they show faith. God can work with our faith; He just cannot work with our doubts and fear. Faith-filled words give God something to work on. It closes the door to the enemy to step in and create havoc.

Do not only speak faith-filled words in your own situation but also speak them when encouraging others. Two stories are not the same - the outcomes are not the same. So, when someone comes to you for encouragement in the pursuit of their purpose, encourage them. Do not just encourage them with empty words. Use the word of God to encourage them so they can have a solid foundation to rely on. Remember that the word of God is life.

Application

How can you speak words of faith?

- *Look through the bible and select 2-3 bible verses that speak to you directly and write those down. Every morning and throughout the day, read those verses out loud. As such you will get into the habit of speaking words of faith and encouragement.*

- *If you are a mentor or leader, and someone comes to*

you for direction in the pursuit of their purpose, do not use your words to discourage. For example, if someone wants to start a business and comes to you for advice, provide the facts while ensuring that you are not using negative words to discourage them. Recognize their efforts, while pointing out the risks. I always say there is no business without risks; you just have to develop strategies on mitigating them.

CHAPTER 6

CAN TWO WALK TOGETHER UNLESS THEY HAVE AGREED?

Amos 3:3

> Can two walk together, unless they have agreed to meet?

In the journey of discovering and pursing our purpose, sometimes God gives us partners with whom we must walk together to attain our purpose. These partners could be spouses, friends, siblings, coworkers, etc. The success of these partnerships depends on the focus and commitment of everyone to the mission. Sometimes, partners are committed at the beginning of the journey; but then somewhere along the line, their commitments shift, and the partnership is broken.

৵ ৵ ৵

The Start of a Partnership: Germany 2007

It is 3 a.m. and my boyfriend and I are rushing to catch the bus that would get us to the Hauptbahnhof (Train station) where we'll catch a train to a warehouse facility. There, we would be assigned along with other students to a machine to sort and load boxes of bottles on a palette. The work was hard manual labor, but it paid the bills and enabled us to take care of family back in Cameroon. We had come as foreign students in Germany. Though we were only allowed to work on a limited number of days and during short holiday breaks, we found a way to work all round, sacrificing our education for survival. We never lacked hope for a better tomorrow. We had plans to start a family and to establish a business back in Africa. We were in love and believed that our love was strong enough to withstand the storms. We encouraged each other when we were tired; we were partners. Our ideas were limitless, and our hope vibrant. We were willing and prepared to do what it takes to make our plans work. Our commitment and faith were strong; and as such we braved the hardship, the lack, and the pain together as partners.

The End of The Partnership: USA 2009

The move to the US in 2009 came as a blessing, an open door to the accomplishment of our plans and projects. The birth of our daughter crowned the partnership. Finally, an opportunity to see our various projects come to live. But then things did not turn out the way we had expected. At least, not the way I had expected. Our commitments had shifted. We were no longer in agreement. An intercepted email shed light on an affair which ultimately destroyed the foundations of our partnership. My partner had not only been found cheating but was also expecting a baby. My world fell apart. My heart was broken into pieces. It was almost as if someone had pierced my heart with a sword. I had never felt such pain before. All our dreams were broken and each of us went their separate ways. The partnership had been destroyed.

ॐ ॐ ॐ

Partnerships can make or break our purpose. Before entering into any form and type of partnership, we need prayers and directions from God. Oftentimes, we do not spend sufficient time to pray for direction before entering into partnership with others. Our purpose is too important to not put in enough consideration as to the partnerships we are forming. Wrong partnerships can distort the purpose just as right partnerships can lead to open doors and unlimited possibilities. Partners bring to the team something different and unique about them. They each bring their talents, experiences, skills and abilities and together can move the vision forward. Partners also bring negative aspects of themselves, such as laziness, procrastination, lack of integrity, etc. Hence the necessity to beware of all these factors before entering into any form of partnership especially one that is to fulfill one's purpose.

What does a successful partnership look like? The story of Ruth and Naomi is an example of a partnership that fulfilled purpose.

The Story of Naomi and Ruth: Ruth 1:11-18

But Naomi said, "Turn back my daughters, why will

you go with me? Have I yet sons in my womb that they may become your husbands? Turn back, my daughters; go your way; for I am too old to have a husband. If I should say I have hope even if I should have a husband tonight and should bear sons, would you therefore wait till they were grown? Would you therefore refrain from marrying? No, my daughters, for it is exceedingly bitter to me for your sake that the hand of the Lord has gone out against me." Then they lifted up their voices and wept again. And Orpah kissed her mother-in-law, but Ruth clung to her.

Naomi's life took a twisted turn when she became a widow and lost her two sons. Stuck in a foreign land with no options, she made the decision to return to her native land. She instructed her daughters-in-law to return to their homes. But Ruth clung to her. At this point, the ties between Naomi and Ruth were broken by the death of her son and Ruth's husband. Ruth had no obligation to remain with Naomi. But she did. Ruth was faithful. Faithful to the mission. Faithful until death.

And she said, "See your sister-in-law has gone back to her people and her gods; return after your sister-in-law." But Ruth said, "Don't urge me to leave you or to return from following you. For where you go, I will go, and where you lodge, I will lodge. Your people shall be my people, and your God my God. Where you die, I will die, and there I will be buried. May the Lord do so to me and more also if anything but death parts me from you." When Naomi saw that she was determined to go with her, she said no more.

Most often, when people are ready to get into a partnership; they do not spend time in prayer to seek wisdom from God. Nor do they spend time studying their would-be partner to know if he/she has the required characteristics of a kingdom partner. Not all partnerships are for good. Not all partnerships are kingdom-based and ordained by God. In the pursuit of our purpose, it is of utmost importance to connect with others who have been ordained by God to work with us in the fulfilment of the purpose. Who is a kingdom partner? It is someone who has been placed in your life to support you to pursue your purpose. They bring in a different set of skills, abilities and experiences to the table. Before entering into a partnership with someone, it is important to ask the question- is this a kingdom partner?

Ruth demonstrated the four characteristics of a Kingdom Partner:

1. Fear of God. The bible tells us that the fear of God is the beginning of wisdom. For two to work together, they both must have the fear of God. If you do not fear God, then you will not do what's right. You will not act with integrity. It is important to know the beliefs of the person with whom you are entering into a partnership. God must be at the center of it all.

2. Commitment to the purpose and willingness to run the race to the end, regardless of the outcome. A kingdom partner is one that understands that this is about God's glory.

3. Shared values - your kingdom partner should have the same values as you. There should be compatible

values. And both of you should be aware of what are some of the things you can compromise on and what you cannot.

4. Complement of skills and abilities. God has given all of us a set of talents. No one has it all. I may be horrible in numbers but good in policies. I would need a partner who is good in numbers, so that both our talents can complement each other for the glory of God.

The mission of a partnership is to accomplish the God-given task. Before entering a partnership with someone, we should ask ourselves if the partnership is from God and if the person/ people demonstrate the characteristics displayed by Ruth. It doesn't matter the nature of the partnership; it could be a marriage, a business relationship, etc., either way we need to be observant while at the same time checking ourselves to make sure we remain committed to the purpose of the partnership. Doing our fact-finding steps early on before entering into a partnership saves us time and pain from the consequences of a wrong partnership.

The story of Naomi and Ruth is a story of a successful partnership, which was rewarded by Ruth getting married to Boaz and having a son. This marriage gave Naomi and Ruth not only financially stability and a family (both of which they had lost in the foreign land); it also made them to be part of the lineage of Jesus. Ruth's son and Naomi's grandson was Obed, the father of Jesse, who was the father of King David. This story just goes to show what benefits are found when one is in the right type of partnership. The fulfillment of purpose might require you to build partnerships with others.

It is important for you to be observant as to what the Lord is saying, not only about your partners but about the partnership. We should not get into partnerships like those with no knowledge of their God. We should not also be proud and think we can achieve all by ourselves. Oftentimes we need the skills, abilities and talents of the other person to fulfill our purpose.

Application

- *List 5 values that are most important to you. Does your partner possess any of those values? For example, if you value being proactive, does your partner have the tendency to procrastinate? If that is the case, find ways to work on the weak points. Do not ignore them. It could prove to be critical when working on time-sensitive projects.*

CHAPTER 7

FAITH FOR TWO

It is 2017. I am showing my mother around the new space for our center to support adults with intellectual disability. My mother walked around the empty 1800 square footage space with a look of distress, sorrow, and disapproval. Upon returning to our car, she said: "I hope that this business is just a side business. You still have to keep your main job because you can never trust a business to sustain you."

My mother's words sank deep in me but found no ground because I had seen what the Lord had done in my life to get me to this point and I had no doubt that I was answering His call for my life.

So, a few months later, when I finally quit my secure State job, I did not tell my mom. I got up every morning and got ready for work but there was no work; only an empty business space. I occupied this space for weeks, wondering when the doors would open, wondering when the first clients would flood in. Day in, day out, as I stared into the empty space my spirit was calm, and I was not afraid. The Lord comforted me and sustained me as I waited for the manifestation of what

He had promised. I did as King David; I encouraged myself in the Lord using bible verses and praises.

Many of us are waiting to do what God has asked us to do because we are expecting and waiting on others - family members, loved ones, spouses, etc. to support us and demonstrate the same faith as we have or even more faith to sustain our lack of faith or weak faith. But the vision was not given to them - it was given to you. When times get rough and we cannot seem to get the support from others, we need to encourage ourselves in the Lord.

Sometimes We Need to Have Faith For Two

The Bible recounts in Numbers chapters 13 and 14 the story of the spies and the promised land. The Lord instructed Moses to send out spies, among which were Joshua and Caleb, to go spy in Canaan, the promised land. Moses gave the spies specific instructions (Numbers 13:17-22). At the end of the forty days, the spies returned with mixed reports. Caleb's report was based on faith and full of encouragement. He told the people to go up at once and occupy the land, for they were well able to overcome it. The other spies' report was based on lack of faith, fear, and discouragement. They reported that the people who dwelled on the land were strong and that the land devoured its people. The Israelites, overcome by fear, decided to believe the report of the other spies, and grumbled against the Lord. The Lord decided to punish that generation - they did not enter the promised land. Caleb was blessed to possess the land 40 years later (Joshua 14: 4-14).

A group went to spy and saw two different things. One group saw the land through their eyes of fear whilst the other group saw the same thing through their eyes of faith. The

Israelites were taken by fear and decided to believe the report of the majority. The fear of the majority took control over the crowd.

What does this mean for me?

Sometimes when God calls us into a purpose, we need to be like Caleb and look at it from the lens of faith and encourage ourselves in the Lord. Not everyone would look at the same image, read the same information, collect the same data, and have the same vision for it. There are always two ways of looking at a project - from a place of fear or from a place of faith.

Sometimes, we are the ones called upon to set the direction; to be the pacesetters for our families and our communities by exercising faith for two. Not waiting for others to uplift us but to be the voice of faith that lifts others up; that encourages others and propels them to see beyond the difficulties into the possibilities; not looking upon themselves but upon Christ through which all things are possible. Our faith then serves as a propellant to pull others to follow us. And even if they do not end up following us, we should wait patiently and in faith like Caleb did for the manifestation of God's promise in our lives. Do not let the crowd discourage you from pursuing your purpose. If you are always waiting for cheerleaders to cheer you along the way, you will never make it home.

ৰ ৰ ৰ

Grace: When a Mother Has Faith For Two

When my daughter Grace was 2 years old, we were scheduled for her annual physical; the nurse practitioner asked me how many words she was able to speak. A simple question, so I thought. But one that opened Grace and I to a new world. At 2, Grace could barely articulate two words. What I thought was "normal" was revealed by the nurse practitioner to be abnormal. I was referred to an agency specialized in testing toddlers for autism. That was the first time I ever heard the word autism. Returning home from that annual visit was a living nightmare. I was in a trance. I cried the whole night. I was confused. What was wrong with my little girl? I blamed myself. Was there something I could have done differently?

Grace was diagnosed to have had a speech delay and needed to receive in-house speech therapy sessions. I could see her frustrations when she was attempting to communicate with me about something she needed but all she could do was to point at it while screaming and crying. A family member once made a comment that my daughter was having a speech delay because I was not talking to her often. Other family members made me feel ashamed like there was something wrong with my daughter. In some African contexts, having a speech delay was considered a taboo and looked upon as if something were "wrong" with the child or with the parents. I constantly found myself defending and explaining my daughter's diagnosis. A speech delay was not a fatality. Around other children, I feared for my daughter. I feared that she would be bullied and misunderstood.

But I refused to let what was happening be the final say in my daughter's life. I decided to have a faith for two. In my prayer journal I wrote a simple prayer, "Lord, please I want to talk with my daughter." A simple prayer that was backed with faith and works. It took close to 5 years of intensive speech support for my daughter to speak at a level that was appropriate for her age. God had finally answered my prayers. Today, when I listen to Grace speak, it is hard to believe that there was ever a time she was unable to communicate at a level appropriate for her age.

I had faith for my daughter. I had faith for two. And God in His mercy rewarded that faith and set my daughter on a different path. Sometimes, we may have faith for two and still, our prayers are not being answered. That does not mean God did not hear us or that we have done something wrong. We must keep trusting that God knows why and that His will is always for our good.

Sometimes our purpose in life is to go through a mountain; other times it is to avoid the mountain. Either way, facing our mountains with faith during negative circumstances and others' unbelief is necessary for us to achieve and live a purpose-driven life.

Application

- *Do not face your mountains alone; be part of a prayer group or help group in your local church; Keep in touch with people that care for and about you. Open up so they can help pray for you and encourage you. Write bible verses on stickers and place them on your walls so you can read them each time and encourage yourself.*

CHAPTER 8

COMFORTABLE IN THE BOAT

Sometimes our environment can act as a limiting factor from discovering and pursuing our purpose. In such instances, the environment acts as a boat to constrain us by making us comfortable and limits our vision. To live a purpose-driven life, we must have the courage and faith to step out of the boat. That's Neba's story.

Neba: When Being Bold Pays

Neba's story starts in Bamenda, North West Region of Cameroon. Neba was the first of 7 children. His father was a high school teacher and his mom a seamstress and petty trader in the local market. Growing up, Neba always had dreams of becoming a doctor and being able to take care of his family. But his financial environment constrained him. After graduating from high school in 2000, he enrolled at the University of Yaoundé I. Most of his courses were in the French language and as such Neba struggled to make it through college. But he never gave up. After earning his college degree, Neba was unable to find a job. He returned to Bamenda where he joined his mother in her petty trade business. Just when things seemed like they were not changing, Neba won the US Diversity Visa Lottery and came to the US in 2009.

During his first year in the US, Neba enrolled in the local community college. He wanted to get into the nursing program. So, he started taking prerequisite courses. But the lure of the dollar and the financial pressures of taking care of his siblings and parents pushed Neba to turn his focus on work. Neba found himself working two and sometimes three jobs at the same time. He worked in warehouses, group homes and nursing facilities. School took a backrow seat. For six years, Neba struggled to keep up with school, work, and financial responsibilities. The money from the various jobs was very appealing to Neba. At that time, it did not seem as if Neba could get out of the boat, he had become comfortable.

In 2016, Neba was slated to graduate from the nursing program; but something negative occurred. He was informed by the community college that he could not graduate from the nursing program that semester and needed one more semester to complete the program. Neba was frustrated. He was lost. And that is when the click happened. Neba made the bold decision to step out of the boat; he changed his major to General Studies and graduated that same semester. What he did next was an act of faith and boldness. He sat for the Pharmacy College Admission Test, passed and was admitted into a pharmacy program. For the next three years, Neba concentrated full time in school. At the time, it seemed like 3 years was too long a time. But that time eventually passed. Fast forward to 2020, Neba finally graduated as a Doctor of Pharmacy. Neba was a cycle breaker; he had stepped out of the boat of his circumstances. He had taken a bold step and his courage was rewarded. He had found his purpose.

Sometimes we must all be like Neba, especially when the circumstances of life are holding us captive. We need to take the bold step and refuse to be held back. At the same time that Neba was working in the warehouses, he made friends who had challenges similar to his; they had moved to the area and found very lucrative but hard manual jobs at the warehouses. The money was good, especially with the mandatory overtimes. They found it hard to sacrifice the job and get one with more favorable and limited hours, to pursue an education or training that could set them in a better direction with their lives. Years after Neba left the warehouse and graduated, the same friends he had met at the warehouses were still working minimum pay jobs.

❧ ❧ ❧

The story of the boat in the bible illustrates what happens when we take that bold step and come out of the comfort of the boat. To attain our purpose, we need to be bold and courageous. We need to set ourselves apart and be that cycle-breaker.

Peter steps out of the Boat: Matthew 14: 22-33

> Immediately Jesus made the disciples get into the boat and go before him to the other side, while he dismissed the crowds. And after he had dismissed the crowds, he went up on the mountain by himself to pray. When evening came, he was there alone, but

the boat by this time was a long way from the land, beaten by the waves, for the wind was against them. And in the fourth watch of the night, he came to them, walking on the sea. But when the disciples saw him walking on the sea, they were terrified, and said, "It is a ghost!" and they cried out in fear. But immediately Jesus spoke to them, saying, "Take heart, it is I. Do not be afraid."

And Peter answered him, "Lord, if it is you, command me to come to you on the water."

He said, "Come." So, Peter got out of the boat and walked on the water and came to Jesus. But when he saw the wind, he was afraid, and beginning to sink he cried out, "Lord, save me." Jesus immediately reached out his hand and took hold of him, saying to him, "O you of little faith, why did you doubt?" And when they got into the boat, the wind ceased. And those in the boat worshiped him, saying, "Truly you are the Son of God."

We all have been faced with situations where we have been held back by the boat. What does the boat represent in our lives?

Others' Opinions Of Who We Are

Sometimes friends and family have a limiting opinion of us. They do not see us past a certain level. Sometimes it could be close relations who do not believe we can attain a certain level of education or even financial stability. Their opinions tend to limit us and ultimately affect the way we see ourselves and the way we make use of the opportunities around us. Brothers and sisters limiting each other; parents limiting children; friends limiting each other.

Sometimes these limitations are not our fault but an illustration of who they are; it shows their own fears, insecurities, envies, and shortcomings, which they are trying to push on to somebody else. Other times, we are faced with these limitations because we tend to seek everyone's opinion of our lives and seek everyone's advice before we make any decision. God alone has the final say in our lives. He should be the one we turn to and whose instructions we make haste to obey. We should not look for validation from others. But rely on God first and foremost.

Family limitations are tough to deal with because we cannot run away from loved ones. The pain and disappointment caused by the lack of support or negativity from loved ones is like the cut of a sharp object. It hurts and we bleed. But we need to take a stand and make the decision not to dwell in that boat any longer. To step out of the boat and to be the one who makes the difference in our family. The one who steps up and opens the way for others.

Our Socioeconomic Environment

There is a saying that poverty is a disease, a deadly one for that matter. For it affects not only our physical environment but also attacks our vision and can divert us from pursuing and accomplishing our purpose. Lack of financial means can blind a person not to see beyond the current limitations. It prevents a person from taking risks and damages their hopes.

When you lack the financial means, you tend to look

at an opportunity from the lens of the limitation instead of trusting God. It is said, can a hungry man/woman think about the future?

Our religiosity: some cannot make a move or decide without consulting with their pastors, prophets, men or women of God etc. This opens the room for manipulation and limitations. Manipulations in the form of intentional misinterpretation of information.

The majority: some have made trends their gods. What's trending? One day my daughter was laughing at me because I was not up to date with a trend. So, if it is trending, does it mean it is godly? If we do not follow the trends, does it mean we are lost? Trends can act as limitations if we tend to rely on them for validation to follow our purpose.

Your past: one saying goes thus- when your past comes knocking at the door, do not open because it has nothing to say. How many of us have gotten stuck in the past? Following God's instructions, I travelled for business inquiries in a city I once lived in. Instead of doing what God asked me to do while in the city, I decided to drive around my old neighborhood. I went to my old apartment building, neighborhood stores, library, and the church where my daughter was baptized. The revival of the old and painful memories failed to bring me joy. It brought emptiness. After driving around for an hour, I asked myself what was I thinking? What was I hoping to get by opening that door? I turned to God and sought for directions. He reminded me that He never instructed me to go revisit the past. He reminded me that He called me out of that place to a new place.

What does this mean for me?

Many of us get too comfortable in the boat along with

others doing the same thing. Not going anywhere. Not being courageous enough to step out of the boat and be different. Because difference means everyone else's eyes are on you, watching you, expecting that like Peter, you would fall and sink. But unbeknownst to them, God is standing right there, ready to catch you up. He is waiting for you to take hold of His word and step out of the comfort of the boat, out of past experiences, out of family traditions, out of negative mindsets and step into purpose.

Application

What are some practical steps we can take to step out of the boat of our circumstances?

- *Work on a vision board. Where do you envision yourself in 3 years? 5 years?*

- *Come up with 2-3 options.*

- *Write down short-term goals you can achieve.*

- *Ask for advice; work with a mentor/mentors especially one in the field you want to move into.*

- *Be accountable. Share your goals with others who can hold you accountable and keep you on track. Accountability is key in helping you to make sure you are not too comfortable in the boat. Have trusted people who can check on your progress and encourage or even reprimand you when it appears you are getting too* comfortable in the boat.

- *Finally, be flexible to change plans: change the plans but never the mission.*

CHAPTER 9

DRAW THE LINE IN THE SAND

Growing up, I always heard words that dampen my morale and confidence in my abilities; you are too lazy, you will never succeed, you are too reserved, you are too skinny, you are not smart enough, you have too many friends, you have too few friends, you do not speak to others, you are not sociable enough. Are you sure you can work? It was one thing after the next.

After a trip back to Cameroon from Europe, a family friend asked me how Germany was. I poured myself out, explaining how tough the country was for African students. Her response? I knew you would never make it because you are too lazy. Those words struck a chord in me.

I painfully remember all those long hours working at the warehouses; filling up pallets of products, mounting them on each other and pulling them to the sections to be loaded into the vans. Long hours working in freezing conditions, rolling intestines as salt water spilled on my face and in my eyes. But here I was, accused of being lazy.

For some reason it is always those who know your past

that make derogatory comments about your present and your future. It is always those who knew you when you had nothing who do not believe you can amount to something. People who know your background that despise your purpose. To be able to discover and fulfill your purpose, you need to draw a line in the sand.

Drawing the line in the sand means making the decision that you need to change a situation. Not being happy where you are and deciding to change things. To be specific about what you want and to make the decision to create what you want by surrounding yourself with people who can help you move to the next level. Drawing a line means deciding to step away from your past and changing your outcome – that is to draw a line between who you are and who you want to be.

~ ~ ~

How I Drew The Line in The Sand

It was the fall of 2013 and I was staring out the window of a State office in downtown Pittsburgh, Pennsylvania. I turned to Jo-Jo, my friend and co-worker and said, "Jo-Jo I am relocating to Harrisburg." The news did not really come as a surprise to Jo-jo because she had seen my mood go downhill and had seen my frustrations over the course of 5 months. Indeed, I was frustrated with my current situation. I had obtained a job as a limited-term clerk, processing applications for energy-assistance benefits, while pursuing a Master's in Business Administration at a college, just down the street from where my office was located.

I thought the one-year MBA program was going to open doors of opportunities for me but it had not. Two months to the end of the program, I did not have any meaningful job interviews or offers. The only one I could get were low paying jobs such as bank tellers which were paying less than what I was earning as a clerk for the State.

Prior to obtaining the job as a clerk, I had submitted several unsuccessful applications in several companies. I received the same rejection email: I lacked the required experience. While researching, I came across jobs with the State, which required applicants to take a civil service test if they met the requirements for the jobs. I was excited for that was one area I knew I had experience in - taking tests. So, I signed up for as many civil service tests as possible and was finally able to have a job as a clerk, which for me was the opening step into state jobs. But after working for five months and nearing the end of my MBA program, I came to the sad realization that there were not many state job openings in Allegheny County, beyond clerical ones. I grew frustrated. It felt like I was wasting away. I remember those days when we got few applications for benefits and were instructed by our team leaders to slow the pace down. As such, we would spend the whole 7 hours just processing 5 applications, so as not to run the risk of not having any work to do and losing our temporary jobs.

I felt like I was chained. Like that was going to be my story. But then I decided to draw a line in the sand and take a bold step. I researched and found that many state jobs were in Harrisburg, the capital city of Pennsylvania. So, I sat for a dozen of civil service tests for professional and higher paid positions located in Harrisburg. I did not know anyone in the area, but I was not worried about that. I had made the decision to change things. I was not going to stay in the same place.

Jo-jo was rightfully worried about me venturing into the unknown and not sure about what was going to happen, but she understood my frustrations. Five months after that conversation, I had drawn the line and moved into another city accepting a promotion with the State as a Human Resource Analyst; a job whose pay was more in alignment with my degree.

On my farewell card, a co-worker wrote: "Christine - you broke free." Powerful words. Indeed, I had broken free. I had drawn the line in the sand and had the courage to relocate with my daughter to a new town, with no guarantees. Two months after relocating to Harrisburg, I got a back-to-back promotion. It was as if God was rewarding my courage and faith. Rewarding me for having drawn that line in the sand and taken that critical step.

❧ ❧ ❧

It takes courage to take a step and move away from others' perceptions of who we are; others' knowledge of our past circumstances that are holding us captive, and our circumstances. Sometimes, to move into our purpose, we need to make the decision to depart from our old and former ways. The bible says new wine cannot be poured into old wineskins. We need to be able to draw the line in the sand. The bible has a story of one woman who made a decision and moved from her past into her purpose.

Jesus Writing on the Ground: John 8:1-11

John 8:1-11 tells the story of Jesus and the woman caught in adultery. The scribes and the Pharisees brought the woman and quoting the Law, tried to trick Jesus into stoning her. Instead, he bent down and wrote with his finger on the ground and said. "Let him who is without sin among you be the first to throw a stone at her." But when they heard it, they went away one by one, and Jesus was left alone with the woman. Jesus then said to her, "Woman, where are they? Has no one condemned you?" She said, "No one, Lord." And Jesus said, "Neither do I condemn you, go, and from now on sin no more".

The woman in the story had committed a shameful act, condemned by law. Her detractors knew what the Law of Moses instructed on how to deal with such cases, but they wanted to trap Jesus.

How many times have we indulged in activities, relationships, and conversations that we know we should not indulge in them? How many times have we been like this woman - our sins, shortcomings and failures exposed to the view and mockery of all? How many times have the desires of our hearts been trampled upon and mocked? We have all been this woman at one point in our lives. We know shame. We know dishonor. We know mockery.

The scribes and the Pharisees were confident in their knowledge of the law and in their self-righteousness. What could they possibly they have to do with an adulteress? They were perfect, she was stained. They had the Law, she was empty. They were saved and she was condemned. No, they could not possibly identify with her because they were superior to her.

How many times have you acted like the scribes and the Pharisees? How many times have we placed ourselves on a pedestal and set standards through which we judge others? We have all been the scribes and the Pharisees. We have all considered ourselves of superior brand than our friends and others in our community. We find it difficult to forgive and accept others. Worse, we find it hard to acknowledge our own shortcomings and failures. We hide these behind culture, tradition, and rules.

What did Jesus do? He drew the line in the sand. Jesus is the ultimate Judge. There is no other and there cannot be another. We cannot place ourselves in the position of Judges over our brothers and sisters. Jesus drew the line to bring us over to the other side of forgiveness and righteousness through Him.

What does this mean for me?

When Jesus calls us into purpose, He is not interested in our past, what our accusers say about us, or how we think about ourselves. He draws the line over our past and who we were, so we must cross over and become who He has called us to be. Crossing over means forgiving ourselves and others and acknowledging our shortcomings and failures. Knowing that we cannot become all that He has called us to be on our own. Drawing the line means we move on the other side with Jesus; we forsake old ways of thinking, all sinful and unfruitful habits, all unfruitful and time waster conversations, negativity and move into faith, love and hope for ourselves and for others. Finally, drawing the line means walking with discernment to know when we are on the wrong side and have the humility to move into the other side with Jesus.

Application

- *Decide to change yourself and/or your situation.*

- *Make a visual board and write down what is preventing you from accomplishing a task or an assignment; then write down some of the things friends/family have spoken negatively about you. Next to each negative thing draw a line and write what you would counter it with. If spending time on the phone is what is holding you back from fulfilling your purpose, draw a line and decide to use that time to research or read on the topics that can help you learn more about your purpose or whatever it is you are currently working on.*

CHAPTER 10

ALL YOU NEED IS ALREADY IN YOUR HAND

God has given each of us talents. We all have something in our hands that we can do better than anyone else. Sometimes, this is what helps us to understand what our purpose is. We could be walking around looking for what to do, looking for a solution to some financial problem, when all along the solution to the problem is in our hands.

Maureen: When God Blesses Your Hand And Changes Your Life

When talking about Maureen, I always like to describe her as someone whose hands God has blessed. When she initially moved into the area, she found herself working at warehouses. The job required her to stand long hours, with mandatory overtime. This was taking a toll on her especially as she was in the early stages of her pregnancy. Maureen had gone through the pain of miscarriage before and did not want to go through another pain. But what could she do? She and her husband needed the money. Her husband was also working in a warehouse, sorting mails. Both jobs were taking a toll on their family life and it did not appear like there was a way out. Then Maureen became sick and the doctor warned her about the risk of losing yet another baby if she did not reduce her work hours. What could she do? She felt lost and confused. Her husband's pay could not sustain them; she had to work, but with no degree or other experience, it was almost impossible to get any other jobs that could pay better than the warehouse.

Unable to continue with the warehouse job, Maureen decided to spend some time at a friend's hair salon. Maureen did not know how to braid. She started observing how it was done and started helping the other braiders to finish the ends of the braids. It was tough but she never gave up. Every day she watched and learned how to braid. Little by little each day, she made progress. At the beginning, many thought she was just killing time because she could not get a job; but what she was unaware of was that God was using that time to bless what was in her hands.

Maureen got better each day and customers started appreciating the result. Soon, her friend started paying her for the service. The money came in handy for Maureen and her husband. It enabled them to stay afloat and she was able to work without risking her health and that of the unborn baby. Soon after she gave birth, Maureen was able to continue working at the salon and earning a living, more than what she had earned working at the warehouse. It was amazing to see how her skills developed over the months. Two years after she started working in the salon, Maureen and her husband were able to save enough money and with the help of a loan from a friend, were able to open her own hair salon. This was indeed God using what was in Maureen's hands to bless her and her family.

Most often, just like Maureen, our purpose could be laying dormant in our hands. Until God steps in and orchestrates an interruption in our lives, we might miss out on the opportunities that are within our hands. Sometimes, we might be tempted to neglect what we have in our hands or fall into the comparison trap. What you have in your hand is meant to be a blessing to you and a blessing for others. It is meant for you to discover and live out your purpose.

There was a woman in the bible who faced a difficult financial situation just like Maureen. She was indebted and did not know what else to do to pay off her debts. Then the prophet asked her what was in her hand.

The Widow and the Oil: 2 Kings 4:1-7

> Now the wife of one of the sons of the prophets cried to Elisha, "Your servant my husband is dead, and you know that your servant feared the Lord, but the creditor has come to take my two children to be his slaves." And Elisha said to her, "What shall I do for you? Tell me; what have you in the house?" And she said, "Your servant has nothing in the house except a jar of oil." Then he said, "Go outside, borrow vessels from all your neighbors, empty vessels and not too few. Then go in and shut the door behind yourself and your sons and pour into all these vessels. And when one is full, set it aside." So, she went from him and shut the door behind her and her sons. And as she poured, they brought the vessels to her. When the vessels were full, she said to her son. "Bring me another vessel."

> And he said to her, "There is not another." Then the oil stopped flowing. She came and told the man of God, and he said. "Go, sell the oil and pay your debts, and you and your sons can live on the rest."

The woman in this story was faced with a challenging situation. Her husband, who had been the servant of the Most High was dead and creditors were threatening to sell off her two children to pay off their debts. She was at her wits' end. She told Elisha she only had a jar of oil. At this point, that jar did not have any value in her eyes. There was no way anything good could come from that jar. The jar was too insignificant and small to pay off the debts. It did not possess any value in her eyes.

What came next must have been a shock to the woman. The prophet gave her firm instructions. She was to borrow empty vessels from her neighbors, shut the door behind her, and pour the oil in the vessels until there was none left, and sell the oil to pay her debts and live on the rest. The woman did as she was instructed. Suddenly the oil had value.

Maybe the lady was expecting Elisha to give her some money. Either way, she probably was not expecting the solution to her problems to be found in her empty house. Nevertheless, she obeyed the instructions and did as she was told by faith. What resulted was not only freedom from debt but financial blessings for her and her children.

It is imperative when God gives us instructions, that we follow them in trust and obedience. Our past experience with God; the battles He won for us, the illness He cured, the accidents He protected us against, and the times He provided for us and our loved ones, and the many times He answered our prayers should act as a testimony to help us stand firm when faced with new battles and challenges. They should act as an encouragement for us not to doubt God. When we get into the habit of constantly reminding ourselves of what God did in the past, we can gather courage and boldness to step into what He is asking of us today.

God has gifted each of us with unique talents, skills, and abilities. But sometimes we fall into the trap of dismissing what we have in our hands. Either because it is not fanciful enough, does not meet ours and others' expectations; does not come adorned in bright and beautiful coverings, etc. Sometimes our eyes could be closed to see the value of the gifts that we have.

The Gift of Writing

I never knew I had the gift to write. It all started when I was asked to lead one of the home fellowships groups at my church. The previous leaders, a couple of college professors, were relocating. During the time they led the group, they had gotten into the habit of summarizing our lessons and discussions at the end of each meeting and posting these on our group platform. I enjoyed reading the summaries. So, when I took over the leadership of the group, I followed the pre-established pattern. Years went by and I kept the practice. Then I found myself actively looking forward to summarizing our lessons and discussions, and I started adding some words and new insights as I was led by the Holy Spirit. Soon I was writing summaries of other church sermons and posting them on the other church groups. I had no clue about the power of the words I was writing, until I started getting positive feedback and encouragement to write more often.

I started writing tracks, and then finally took the bold step of faith to write a book. All along, I never knew the gift was in my hands. I thought I was just continuing a practice, but God was orchestrating everything behind the scenes to bring me to my purpose. Since then, I use my writing to encourage and minister to others.

Today, make the decision to ask God to reveal what is in your hand. Be willing to step out and obey the instructions. The solution to that problem and the breakthrough could be closer to home than you know. All you need is for God to open your eyes and show you. All you need are the instructions from God.

Elisha gave instructions to the widow and a miracle took place. When God gives you instructions on how to use the gifts, talents and experiences you have in your hand, then the breakthrough occurs. The purpose starts getting fulfilled.

Another story in the bible, where someone used what he had in this hand to fulfill his purpose was the story of David.

David was a shepherd boy. His job was considered insignificant by his father and his brothers. They neglected what David had in his hands. When Samuel visited David's home and wanted to anoint one of them as the next King of Israel, Jesse, his father didn't send for him until Samuel requested he be fetched, for they were not going to sit down until he came. Even after Samuel anointed David as King, David was still left to tend the sheep. During the battle with the Philistines and while his brothers followed Saul, David was left to tend his father's sheep, until the appointed time came when he was thrust into the limelight to pursue his purpose.

To defeat Goliath, David had to rely on what was his hand. He told Saul:

"Your servant used to keep sheep for his father. And then there came a lion, or a bear, and took a lamb from the flock, I went after him and struck him and delivered it out of his mouth. And if it arose against me, I caught him by his beard and struck him and killed him. Your servant had struck down both lions and bears, and this uncircumcised Philistine shall be like one of them, for he has defied the armies of the living God." and David said, "the Lord who delivered me from the paw of the lion and from the paw of the bear will deliver me from the hand of this Philistine." And Saul said to David, "Go, and the Lord be with you." *1 Samuel 17: 34-37.*

David was not ashamed of what was in his hand. He used his experience as a steppingstone into his purpose. He used what God had done to him in the past as an encouragement for what he was going to do in the present. David did not only have trust in God, but he also had confidence in his skills and abilities. David defeated Goliath using a tool he had in his hand which had served him while he tendered his father's sheep in the field. Never underestimate the power of what is in your hands.

A skill and a gift left unused dies. Make a conscious decision to use what is in your hand and obey God's instructions; irrespective of the platform you find yourself. You must be ready and prepared to move from the training place to the limelight, from behind the scenes to the front stage. It does not matter what the stage is, you should use your gift in the same capacity. Do not strive for the limelight. At the appointed time, God himself will set the stage for the manifestation of your gifting.

Application

- *Ask trusted friends for a list of some of the things they admire about you; your strong points and those things you do best. You would be surprised to discover some skills you were unaware you possessed.*

- *Write your own list of things you enjoy doing and compare both lists. The similar traits are your strengths and what is in your hands.*

- *Sign up to volunteer or mentor someone in any capacity that helps you to utilize the skills you have identified from number 1 and 2 above.*

- *Trust God to reveal what is in your hand and what your purpose is as you go through the process.*

CHAPTER 11

LEAN NOT ON YOUR OWN UNDERSTANDING

Sometimes when God gives us an assignment or a purpose, we might be tempted to follow our own course and lean on our own understanding. We erroneously think we know all the details about the assignment and as such run along with our ignorance until we hit a dead end. I found myself in this position when God led me to open a center to support adults with intellectual disabilities.

I needed a space that was compliant with the regulations. So, I started searching various spaces for rent. I did the preliminary research of what specifications the space needed to meet the Uniform Commercial Code (UCC) requirements. Unbeknownst to me at the time, I was reading an outdated UCC document.

I found a space I thought would meet the requirements. Looking at the space through my human lens, I rejoiced at the idea of having found the perfect space. I did not bother to go back to God and ask for His approval. I contacted the UCC municipal agent, who had to inspect the space and give me the green light. He gave me an appointment for the following week. Instead of waiting for the inspection, I hurriedly met with the landlord and arranged to sign the lease. I was convinced that the space would pass the test and meet the requirements. On the day of the lease signing, I had an uneasiness in my stomach. But I waved it away as fear. There was no way that space could not meet the requirements. Everything was perfect. I convinced myself that this uneasy feeling had to be fear. Be gone fear, I kept repeating to myself.

So, I signed the lease. On the following Monday, the UCC Municipal Agent called me and informed me that he had looked at the building plans from the municipality (no need to physically check the building) and that the building in its current state couldn't meet the requirements. An overhaul of the structural design of the building was needed, which was going to cost tens of thousands of dollars. Money that I did not have.

My world fell into pieces. Here I was with a signed lease for a space I could not use because I had hurriedly ran with what I thought was the right path. I had failed to get an approval from God. I had leaned on my own understanding. It took the grace of God to deliver me from that situation. I ultimately found a better place while working with God and following His lead.

The bible shares the story of a king who leaned on his own understanding and saw the kingdom taken away from him.

Saul and Samuel: 1 Samuel 13:3-14

> Jonathan attacked the Philistine outpost at Geba, and the Philistines heard about it. Then Saul had the

trumpet blown throughout the land and said, "Let the Hebrews hear!" So all Israel heard the news: "Saul has attacked the Philistine outpost, and now Israel has become obnoxious to the Philistines." And the people were summoned to join Saul at Gilgal.

The Philistines assembled to fight Israel, with three thousand chariots, six thousand charioteers, and soldiers as numerous as the sand on the seashore. They went up and camped at Mikmash, east of Beth Aven. When the Israelites saw that their situation was critical and that their army was hard pressed, they hid in caves and thickets, among the rocks, and in pits and cisterns. Some Hebrews even crossed the Jordan to the land of Gad and Gilead.

Saul remained at Gilgal, and all the troops with him were quaking with fear. He waited seven days, the time set by Samuel; but Samuel did not come to Gilgal, and Saul's men began to scatter. So he said, "Bring me the burnt offering and the fellowship offerings." And Saul offered up the burnt offering. Just as he finished making the offering, Samuel arrived, and Saul went out to greet him.

"What have you done?" asked Samuel.

Saul replied, "When I saw that the men were scattering, and that you did not come at the set time, and that the Philistines were assembling at Mikmash, I thought, 'Now the Philistines will come down against

me at Gilgal, and I have not sought the Lord's favor.'
So, I felt compelled to offer the burnt offering."

"You have done a foolish thing," Samuel said. "You
have not kept the command the Lord your God
gave you; if you had, he would have established
your kingdom over Israel for all time. But now your
kingdom will not endure; the Lord has sought out a
man after his own heart and appointed him ruler of
his people, because you have not kept the Lord's
command."

This biblical passage brings to light some key points:
impatience, fear and misunderstanding of the instructions
leading to disobedience. Saul had received fixed instructions
from God to wait for Samuel to perform the sacrifice. Saul
waited for Samuel for seven days as instructed. But then, Saul
became impatient and afraid as he saw the crowd departing
from him. He disobeyed the instructions and thought that
he could perform the burnt offering himself. He relied on
his own understanding.

Sometimes we act like Saul. We have received fixed
instructions from God either through His word, visions or
through others; but we get carried away by what is happening
in the physical. We let fear come in and take a seat in our
minds and thoughts. We believe we can sort the issue by our
own power and understanding.

It is important that we always cross check our actions and
make sure we are not leaning on our own understanding but
are obeying God's instructions. How do we know we are not
leaning on our own understanding?

A famous woman of God once said, "If you don't know what to do, keep doing the last thing God told you to do." In this case, Saul was supposed to keep doing the last thing God told him to do, which was to wait for Samuel to come and offer the burnt offering.

Leaning on our own understanding has also to do with control. When God calls us into a purpose or an assignment, He most often does not show us the whole picture. If God had shown to Saul that the Philistines were going to multiply their numbers and that consequently the people were going to scatter, Saul probably would have been mentally prepared and would have waited for Samuel.

Unfortunately, that is not how it happens. Most of the time God shows us a piece of the puzzle and expects us to run with it in faith. We are to continue doing what He asked us to do while waiting to hear from Him for new directions. When we get to the crossroads, where we need to make a decision, we should return to God and seek His approval.

The story of Noah and the ark is a perfect example of patiently following God's instructions. Noah, who had never witnessed a flood before was tasked by God to build an ark with specific instructions. Noah had to patiently follow God's directions. He probably went back to God several times in prayer for further directions. The directions might have come in bits and pieces and Noah had to rely on hearing from God to know which steps to take.

Listerning and hearing from God comes through practice and intentionally turning to God for directions before we decide. We should get into the habit of listening to God's voice during the chaos and distractions in our daily lives. Listening to Him is an important element of being in His will and pursuing our purpose. As the bible says, partial obedience is disobedience. Just as Saul could not argue that he had waited for Samuel for seven days before deciding to perform the sacrifice himself, so too we have no justification when we partially obey God.

Just like Noah, most of the assignments for which God has called us, would be new to us and seem like an insurmountable task. As such it is imperative for us to get into the habit of listerning to God's instructions. The bible says, ask and you will receive. Get into the habit of asking for wisdom when stuck in a difficult situation. God will share the next steps to you. He wants you to succeed in your calling and in your purpose. He never meant for you to do it on your own. He is always willing to help you and show you the next step, but you must get into the habit of not only asking but also dwelling in His presence to hear the answer

What does this mean for me?

Proverbs 3: 5-8

> Trust in the Lord with all your heart, and do not lean on your own understanding. In all your ways acknowledge him, and he will make straight your paths. Be wise in your own eyes; fear the Lord and turn away from evil. It will be healing to your flesh and refreshment to your bones.

God is faithful to complete whatever work he assigned you to do. He is more than capable of bringing it to completion. All He asks of you is to trust and obey. No matter how long and tedious the walk is; if we stay the course, patiently waiting to hear from Him, obeying the last instructions He gave us, trusting in the promises of His word, not looking at the dangers around us with physical eyes but with our eyes of faith, then God will come through and oh, how wonderful it will be.

Application

- *What can you do when you need to make a decision but are unsure? Seek advice and counsel from trusted sources. Get two to three opinions over the decision you need to make. Speak to those who have experience and knowledge in what you are trying to accomplish and learn from their past mistakes. If in business, seek to be mentored by someone who has succeeded in establishing and sustaining a business.*

EPILOGUE

A s I write this book, the world is hit with the Covid-19 global pandemic. It has been almost one week since businesses and schools shut down, including my businesses. Fear has gripped the nations. People are hoarding supplies; food, toilet rolls, water, etc.; people are living in fear, isolated or quarantined in their homes. The fear of death is lingering on. The fear of uncertainty has held the land and its inhabitants captives.

As I sit looking at my computer, I wonder if a book on discovering your purpose is relevant in times like these. I battle with my own faith. I wonder what the end would look like. Especially with the uncertainty of how long the pandemic and the shutdown would last. I am constantly on news channels, keeping up to date with the pandemic, trying to understand the non-understandable, trying to make sense out of the senseless, trying to be the first to grasp a glimpse of the end.

Is a book on discovering your purpose relevant in times like these?

The answer is yes! But why you might ask.

In everything I give God glory that I was able to discover my purpose. I give God glory that He let me use my talents for His glory and as such come to a state of fulfilment, of happiness and joy. The shutdown has only stressed the importance of discovering and living out one's purpose when given the time and the opportunity. Because one thing is sure, this world and all that is in it would come to an end someday. It might not be today. But it will someday. As a good friend of mine always says, "We are each walking around with numbers in our pockets, we do not know when our numbers would be called, but we know without doubt that they will be called one day."

So how do you want to live your life while waiting for that day when your number will be called? That is the million-dollar question each of us has to answer.

May this shutdown enable us to appreciate life more and place value on those things that have eternal value. May it prompt us to channel our focus on discovering our purpose and give God glory by so doing. So, we too can hear at the end of it all the most precious words ever: *"Well done, good and faithful servant." Matthew 25:23*

ABOUT THE AUTHOR

Christine Titih is the founder and President of Oaks of Central PA, a 501 c3 not-for-profit whose mission is to empower, promote and advocate for the African immigrant and refugee community in the Greater Harrisburg area. She is also the CEO of CT Home Care Services, which provides home and community-based services to adults with physical and intellectual disabilities.

Christine is originally from Bali in the North West region of Cameroon. She holds an MBA in International Business from Point Park University, Pittsburgh, PA. She lives in Camp Hill, PA with her daughter and mother.

ABOUT THE PUBLISHER

Spears Books is an independent publisher dedicated to providing innovative publication strategies with emphasis on African/Africana stories and perspectives. As a platform for alternative voices, we prioritize the accessibility and affordability of our titles in order to ensure that relevant and often marginal voices are represented at the global marketplace of ideas. Our titles – poetry, fiction, narrative nonfiction, memoirs, reference, travel writing, African languages, and young people's literature – aim to bring African worldviews closer to diverse readers. Our titles are distributed in paperback and electronic formats globally by African Books Collective.

Connect with Us

Visit our Website

Go to www.spearsmedia.com to learn about exclusive previews and read excerpts of new books, find detailed information on our titles, authors, subject area books, and special discounts.

Subscribe to our Free Newsletter

Be amongst the first to hear about our newest publications, special discount offers, news about bestsellers, author interviews, coupons and more! Subscribe to our newsletter by visiting www.spearsmedia.com

Quantity Discounts

Spears Books are available at quantity discounts for orders of ten or more copies. Contact Spears Books at orders@spearsmedia.com.

Host a Reading Group

Learn more about how to host a reading group on our website at www.spearsmedia.com

ABOUT THE BOOK

How can so many appear to be living an accomplished life but still feel empty inside? Why are some still marking time on the same spot, doing the same unfulfilling tasks and unable to break the cycle? What prevents us from taking the necessary steps towards changing our condition? Christine Titih approaches these questions with astounding simplicity and forceful conviction. Punctuated with powerful stories about her life, friends and family, including key biblical passages, she guides us eloquently on a discovery of our purpose and how to find happiness amidst the limitations, uncertainties and deprivations that encumber our lives. How I Discovered my Purpose provides precise and practical instruction with applications suitable for our times and for those stormy days when hope is rare to find.

www.ingramcontent.com/pod-product-compliance
Lightning Source LLC
Chambersburg PA
CBHW030155100526
44592CB00009B/281